Robert Stephen Hawker, C. E. (Charles Edward) Byles

Cornish Ballads With Other Poems

Robert Stephen Hawker, C. E. (Charles Edward) Byles

Cornish Ballads With Other Poems

ISBN/EAN: 9783744777629

Printed in Europe, USA, Canada, Australia, Japan

Cover: Foto ©Thomas Meinert / pixelio.de

More available books at **www.hansebooks.com**

THE CORNISH BALLADS

With other Poems

BY THE LATE

REV. R. S. HAWKER,

VICAR OF MORWENSTOW:

Including a New Edition of "The Quest of the Sangraal."

SECOND EDITION.

Parker and Co.
OXFORD, AND 6 SOUTHAMPTON-STREET,
STRAND, LONDON.
1884.

PREFATORY NOTE.

THIS volume is little more than a re-issue of that published in 1869; the Ballads and Poems were selected by the lamented Author, and received his latest corrections. They are the pieces by which his reputation as a Poet will chiefly live in the future, and are mainly connected with the "Tamar Side," the land with which he was, when living, so closely identified, the land of his birth, his life, and his death, "native Cornwall[a]," as he calls it.

The only addition in this new Edition is the Canticle for Christmas, 1874, the Author's last printed, and amongst the most powerful of his lines.

To satisfy the continuous demand for Mr. Hawker's poetical works this volume has now

---

[a] "Quest of the Sangraal," p. 198.

been reprinted, in the hope that it may not be unacceptable to the Public, and attract the attention of readers to whom the Author's writings are but little known.

J. G. G.

July, 1884.

TO

MY DEAR LITTLE DAUGHTERS,

MORWENNA PAULINE AND ROSALIND HAWKER,

I DEDICATE THESE PAGES.

R. S. H.

CONTENTS.

	PAGE
The Song of the Western Men	1
The Silent Tower of Bottreau	3
The Sisters of Glen Nectan	7
A Legend of the Hive	10
The Baptism of the Peasant and the Prince	15
The Wail of the Cornish Mother	19
Dupath Well	21
Annot of Benallay	23
Sir Beville.—The Gate-song of Stowe	26
A Croon on Hennacliff	28
Sir Ralph De Blanc-Minster, of Bien-aimé	31
Mawgan of Melhuach	37
Modryb Marya—Aunt Mary	39
The Doom-Well of St. Madron	41
A Christ-Cross Rhyme	44
The Mystic Magi	46
The Cell	49
The Lost Ship: "The President"	54
The Poor Man and his Parish Church	58
Morwenna Statio	64
The Tamar Spring	68
The Child Jesus	71
The Song of the School: St. Mark's, Morwenstow	73
The Dirge	75
The Storm	77
The Figure-head of the Caledonia at her Captain's Grave	79
Genoveva	81
The Token Stream of Tidna Combe	102
Aishah Schechinah	106
The Lady's Well	110

	PAGE
A Ballad for a Cottage Wall	113
"By the Waters"	116
The Vine	119
The Twain	120
The Well of St. John	121
The Wolf	122
The Saintly Names	123
Clovelly	124
Ephpheta	127
The Signals of Levi	131
The Sea-bird's Cry	137
The Burial Hour	139
The First Prince of Wales	140
The Death-Race	143
The Comet of 1861	146
Absalom's Pillar	148
The Ringers of Lancells Tower	149
Featherstone's Doom	151
Trebarrow	153
Sophie Granville Thynne, on her Fifth Birthday	155
The Lady's Offering	158
"Pater vester pascit illa"	160
"Lord, whither goest Thou?"	161
To Eva Valentine	164
To Matilda Valentine	166
"Blue Eyes melt, dark Eyes burn"	167
Queen Guennivar's Round	168
King Arthur's Waes-hael	170
On the Grave of a Child in Morwenstow Churchyard	172
The Legend of Saint Cecily	173
Saint Thekla	177
The Quest of the Sangraal	180
Pompeii	204
A Canticle for Christmas, 1874	215

The Song of the Western Men.

I.

A GOOD sword and a trusty hand!
    A merry heart and true!
King James's men shall understand
    What Cornish lads can do.

II.

And have they fixed the where and when?
    And shall Trelawny die?
Here's twenty thousand Cornish men
    Will know the reason why!

III.

Out spake their captain brave and bold,
    A merry wight was he:
"If London Tower were Michael's hold,
    We'll set Trelawny free!

IV.

"We'll cross the Tamar, land to land,
    The Severn is no stay,—
With 'one and all,' and hand in hand,
    And who shall bid us nay?

V.

"And when we come to London Wall,
　A pleasant sight to view,
Come forth! Come forth, ye cowards all,
　Here's men as good as you.

VI.

"Trelawny he's in keep and hold,
　Trelawny he may die;—
But here's twenty thousand Cornish bold,
　Will know the reason why!"

NOTE.

With the exception of the choral lines:—
　"And shall Trelawny die?
　Here's twenty thousand Cornish men
　Will know the reason why!"
and which have been ever since the imprisonment, by James the Second, of the seven bishops, one of them Sir Jonathan Trelawny, a popular proverb throughout Cornwall, the whole of this song was composed by me in the year 1825. I wrote it under a stag-horned oak, in Sir Beville's Walk, in Stowe Wood. It was sent by me anonymously to a Plymouth paper, and there it attracted the notice of Mr. Davies Gilbert, who reprinted it at his private press at East Bourne, under the avowed impression that it was the original ballad. It had the good fortune to win the eulogy of Sir Walter Scott, who also deemed it to be the ancient song. It was praised under the same persuasion by Lord Macaulay, and by Mr. Dickens, who inserted it at first as of genuine antiquity in his "Household Words," but who afterwards acknowledged its actual paternity in the same publication.

The Silent Tower of Bottreau.

I.

TINTADGEL bells ring o'er the tide,
The boy leans on his vessel side;
He hears that sound, and dreams of home
Soothe the wild orphan of the foam.
    "Come to thy God in time!"
    Thus saith their pealing chime:
    Youth, manhood, old age past,
    "Come to thy God at last."

II.

But why are Bottreau's echoes still?
Her tower stands proudly on the hill;
Yet the strange chough that home hath found:
The lamb lies sleeping on the ground.
    "Come to thy God in time!"
    Should be her answering chime:
    "Come to thy God at last!"
    Should echo on the blast.

III.

The ship rode down with courses free,
The daughter of a distant sea:
Her sheet was loose, her anchor stored,
The merry Bottreau bells on board.
 "Come to thy God in time!"
 Rung out Tintadgel chime;
 Youth, manhood, old age past,
 "Come to thy God at last!"

IV.

The pilot heard his native bells
Hang on the breeze in fitful swells;
"Thank God," with reverent brow he cried,
"We make the shore with evening's tide."
 "Come to thy God in time!"
 It was his marriage chime:
 Youth, manhood, old age past,
 His bell must ring at last.

V.

"Thank God, thou whining knave, on land,
But thank, at sea, the steersman's hand,"
The captain's voice above the gale:
"Thank the good ship and ready sail."

"Come to thy God in time!"
Sad grew the boding chime:
"Come to thy God at last!"
Boomed heavy on the blast.

VI.

Uprose that sea! as if it heard
The mighty Master's signal-word:
What thrills the captain's whitening lip?
The death-groans of his sinking ship.
"Come to thy God in time!"
Swung deep the funeral chime:
Grace, mercy, kindness past,
"Come to thy God at last!"

VII.

Long did the rescued pilot tell—
When gray hairs o'er his forehead fell,
While those around would hear and weep—
That fearful judgment of the deep.
"Come to thy God in time!"
He read his native chime:
Youth, manhood, old age past,
His bell rung out at last.

VIII.

Still when the storm of Bottreau's waves,
Is wakening in his weedy caves:
Those bells, that sullen surges hide,
Peal their deep notes beneath the tide:
"Come to thy God in time!"
Thus saith the ocean chime:
Storm, billow, whirlwind past,
"Come to thy God at last!"

The Sisters of Glen Nectan.

I.

It is from Nectan's mossy steep,
The foamy waters flash and leap :
It is where shrinking wildflowers grow,
They lave the nymph that dwells below.

II.

But wherefore in this far-off dell,
The reliques of a human cell ?
Where the sad stream and lonely wind
Bring man no tidings of his kind.

III.

" Long years agone :" the old man said,
'Twas told him by his grandsire dead ;
" One day two ancient sisters came :
None there could tell their race or name ;

IV.

"Their speech was not in Cornish phrase,
Their garb had signs of loftier days;
Slight food they took from hands of men,
They withered slowly in that glen.

V.

"One died—the other's sunken eye
Gushed till the fount of tears was dry;
A wild and withering thought had she,
'I shall have none to weep for me.'

VI.

"They found her silent at the last,
Bent in the shape wherein she passed:
Where her lone seat long used to stand,
Her head upon her shrivelled hand."

VII.

Did fancy give this legend birth?
The grandame's tale for winter hearth:
Or some dead bard, by Nectan's stream,
People these banks with such a dream.

VIII.

We know not: but it suits the scene,
To think such wild things here have been:
What spot more meet could grief or sin
Choose, at the last to wither in?

NOTE.

IN a rocky gorge, midway between the castles of Bottreau and Dundagel, there is a fall of waters into a hollow cauldron of native stone, which has borne for ten centuries the name of St. Nectan's Kieve. He was the brother of St. Morwenna, and like her was one of the storied names along this northern shore. He founded the Stations, now the Churches, of Hartland and Wellcombe; and bequeathed his name to other sacred places by the "Severn Sea," in the former ages of Cornish faith.

When I first visited his Kieve in 1830, the outline of an oratory, or the reliques of a cell, stood by the brook, on a knoll, just where the waters took their leap. There was a local legend linked with this ruined abode, which was told me on the spot: and which I expanded at the time into the above ballad. I have recognised the coinage of my brain in the prosaic paraphrase of Wilkie Collins, Walter White, and other subsequent writers; but with regard to any claimant for the original imagination, I must reply in the language of Jack Cade, "No, no; I invented it myself."

A Legend of the Hive.

I.

BEHOLD those wingèd images,
   Bound for their evening bowers:
They are the nation of the bees,
   Born from the breath of flowers.
Strange people they! a mystic race,
In life, and food, and dwelling-place.

II.

They first were seen on earth, 'tis said,
   When the rose breathes in spring:
Men thought her blushing bosom shed
   These children of the wing:
But lo! their hosts went down the wind,
Filled with the thoughts of God's own mind.

III.

They built them houses made with hands,
   And there alone they dwell:
No man to this day understands
   The mystery of their cell.
Your mighty sages cannot see
The deep foundations of the bee.

IV.

Low in the violet's breast of blue,
    For treasured food they sink:
They know the flowers that hold the dew,
    For their small race to drink.
They glide—King Solomon might gaze
With wonder on their aweful ways.

V.

And once—it is a grandame's tale,
    Yet filled with secret lore—
There dwelt within a woodland vale,
    Fast by old Cornwall's shore,
An ancient woman worn and bent,
Fallen nature's mournful monument.

VI.

A home had they,—the clustering race,
    Beside her garden wall:
All blossoms breathed around the place,
    And sunbeams fain would fall.
The lily loved that combe the best
Of all the valleys of the west.

VII.

But so it was, that on a day
    When summer built her bowers,
The waxen wanderers ceased to play
    Around the cottage flowers.
No hum was heard, no wing would roam:
They dwelt within their cloistered home.

VIII.

This lasted long—no tongue could tell
    Their pastime or their toil;
What binds the soldier to the cell?
    Who should divide the spoil?
It lasted long—it fain would last,
Till autumn rustled on the blast.

IX.

Then sternly went that woman old,
    She sought the chancel floor,
And there, with purpose bad and bold,
    Knelt down amid the poor.
She took—she hid—that blessèd bread,
That is, what Jesu, Master, said!

X.

She bare it to her distant home,
　　She laid it by the hive :
To lure the wanderers forth to roam,
　　That so her store might thrive.
'Twas a wild wish, a thought unblest,
Some evil legend of the west.

XI.

But lo! at morning tide, a sign
　　For wondering eyes to trace :
They found above the bread, a shrine
　　Reared by the harmless race.
They brought their walls from bud and flower,
They built bright roof and beamy tower.

XII.

Was it a dream? or did they hear,
　　Float from those golden cells,
A sound as of some psaltery near,
　　Or soft and silvery bells ;
A low sweet psalm that grieved within,
In mournful memory of the sin.

XIII.

Was it a dream? 'tis sweet no less:
   Set not the vision free,
Long let the lingering legend bless
   The nation of the bee.
So shall they bear upon their wings
A parable of sacred things.

XIV.

So shall they teach, when men blaspheme,
   Or sacrament or shrine:
That humbler things may fondly dream
   Of mysteries divine;
And holier hearts than his may beat
Beneath the bold blasphemer's feet.

The Baptism of the Peasant and the Prince.

I.

I CLIMBED a poor and narrow stair,
    The prince's christening day—
I sought a cottage bed, for there
    A travailed woman lay.

II.

With covering thin, and scanty vest,
    Her babe was on her arm:
It was the strong love in her breast
    That kept that infant warm.

III.

I came, a country Minister,
    A servant of the Lord;
To bless that mother's child for her
    With water and the Word.

IV.

The dim light struggling o'er the room,
    Scarce reached the lowly bed:
And thus mid woe, and want, and gloom,
    The Sacrament was shed.

V.

Then said I—for the woman smiled,
    As she took back her son,—
"Be glad! for lo! that little child,
    Is 'mong God's children, one.

VI.

"Henceforth it hath a name on high,
    Where blessèd angels shine:
Nay, one will leave his native sky
    To watch this babe of thine.

VII.

"Be glad! this very day they meet,
    In a far loftier scene,
With blessing and with vow to greet
    The offspring of a queen.

VIII.

"Bright faces beam in bannered halls,
    Around the noble boy:
And princes teach the echoing walls
    The glory of their joy.

IX.

"Yet will the self-same words be said,
    Our lips have uttered now;
And water, such as here we shed,
    Must bless that princely brow.

X.

"One cross, the twain shall seal and sign,
    An equal grace be poured:
One faith, one church, one heaven, will join
    The labourer and his lord."

XI.

"Thanks be to God!" in language mild,
    The humble woman said:
"Who sends such kindness to my child
    Here in its mother's bed.

XII.

"And bless our queen with health and grace,
    Hers is a happy reign:
O! one smile of her baby's face
    Pays her for all her pain."

The Wail of the Cornish Mother.

I.

They say 'tis a sin to sorrow,
   That what God doth is best:
But 'tis only a month to-morrow,
   I buried it from my breast.

II.

I know it should be a pleasure,
   Your child to God to send:—
But mine was a precious treasure
   To me and to my poor friend.

III.

I thought it would call me "mother,"
   The very first words it said;
O! I never can love another,
   Like the blessèd babe that's dead.

IV.

Well, God is its own dear Father,
   It was carried to church and blessed:
And our Saviour's arms will gather
   Such children to their rest.

V.

I shall make my best endeavour,
    That my sins may be forgiven :
I will serve God more than ever,
    To meet my child in heaven.

VI.

I will check this foolish sorrow,
    For what God doth is best :—
But O ! 'tis a month to-morrow,
    I buried it from my breast.

Dupath Well.

I.

Hear how the noble Siward died !
The Leech hath told the woeful bride
'Tis vain : his passing hour is nigh,
And death must quench her warrior's eye.

II.

" Bring me," he said, " the steel I wore,
When Dupath spring was dark with gore :
The spear I raised for Githa's glove,
Those trophies of my wars and love."

III.

Upright he sate within the bed,
The helm on his unyielding head :
Sternly he leaned upon his spear,
He knew his passing hour was near.

IV.

" Githa ! thine hand !" how wild that cry,
How fiercely glared his flashing eye ;
" Sound ! herald !" was his shout of pride :
Hear how the noble Siward died.

V.

A roof must shade that storied stream,
Her dying lord's remembered theme:
A daily vow that lady said,
Where glory wreathed the hero dead.

VI.

Gaze, maiden, gaze on Dupath Well,
Time yet hath spared that solemn cell,
In memory of old love and pride:
Hear how the noble Siward died.

Annot of Benallay.

I.

At lone midnight the death-bell tolled,
  To summon Annot's clay:
For common eyes must not behold
  The griefs of Benallay.

II.

Meek daughter of a haughty line,
  Was Lady Annot born:
That light which was not long to shine,
  The sun that set at morn.

III.

They shrouded her in maiden white,
  They buried her in pall;
And the ring he gave her faith to plight
  Shines on her finger small.

IV.

The Curate reads the dead man's prayer
  The silent Leech stands by:
The sob of voiceless love is there,
  And sorrow's vacant eye.

V.

'Tis over. Two and two they tread
    The churchyard's homeward way:
Farewell! farewell! thou lovely dead:
    Thou Flower of Benallay.

VI.

The sexton stalks with tottering limb,
    Along the chancel floor:
He waits, that old man gray and grim,
    To close the narrow door.

VII.

"Shame! shame! these rings of stones and
    gold!"
    The ghastly caitiff said;
"Better that living hands should hold,
    Than glisten on the dead."

VIII.

The evil wish wrought evil deed,
    The pall is rent away:
And lo! beneath the shattered lid,
    The Flower of Benallay.

IX.

But life gleams from those opening eyes,
    Blood thrills that lifted hand :
And aweful words are in her cries,
    Which none may understand.

X.

Joy! 'tis the miracle of yore,
    Of the city called Nain :—
Lo! glad feet throng the sculptured floor,
    To hail their dead again.

XI.

Joy in the halls of Benallay,
    A stately feast is spread :
Lord Harold is the bridegroom gay,
    The bride th' arisen dead.

Sir Beville.—The Gate-song of Stowe.

I.

Arise! and away! for the King and the land;
   Farewell to the couch and the pillow:
With spear in the rest, and with rein in the hand,
   Let us rush on the foe like a billow.

II.

Call the hind from the plough, and the herd from the fold,
   Bid the Wassailer cease from his revel:
And ride for old Stowe, where the banner's unrolled,
   For the cause of King Charles and Sir Beville.

III.

Trevanion is up, and Godolphin is nigh:
   And Harris of Hayne's o'er the river;
From Lundy to Looe, "One and all" is the cry,
   And The King and Sir Beville for ever.

IV.

Aye! by Tre, Pol, and Pen, ye may know Cornish men,
    'Mid the names and the nobles of Devon;—
But if truth to the King be a signal, why then
    Ye can find out the Granville in heaven.

V.

Ride! ride! with red spur, there is death in delay,
    'Tis a race for dear life with the devil;
If dark Cromwell prevail, and the King must give way,
    This earth is no place for Sir Beville.

VI.

So at Stamford he fought, and at Lansdoune he fell,
    But vain were the visions he cherished:
For the great Cornish heart, that the King loved so well,
    In the grave of the Granville it perished.

A Croon on Hennacliff[a].

I.

Thus said the rushing raven,
    Unto his hungry mate,—
"Ho! gossip! for Bude Haven:
    There be corpses six or eight.
Cawk! cawk! the crew and skipper,
    Are wallowing in the sea:
So there's a savoury supper
    For my old dame and me."

II.

"Cawk! gaffer! thou art dreaming,
    The shore hath wreckers bold;
Would rend the yelling seamen,
    From the clutching billows hold.
Cawk! cawk! they'd bound for booty
    Into the dragon's den:
And shout, for 'death or duty,'
    If the prey were drowning men."

[a] Published in "All the Year Round."

III.

Loud laughed the listening surges,
  At the guess our grandame gave:
You might call them Boanerges,
  From the thunder of their wave.
And mockery followed after
  The sea-bird's jeering brood:
That filled the skies with laughter,
  From Lundy Light to Bude.

IV.

"Cawk! cawk!" then said the raven,
  "I am fourscore years and ten:
Yet never in Bude Haven,
  Did I croak for rescued men.—
They will save the Captain's girdle,
  And shirt, if shirt there be:
But leave their blood to curdle,
  For my old dame and me."

V.

So said the rushing raven,
  Unto his hungry mate,—
"Ho! gossip! for Bude Haven:
  There be corpses six or eight.

Cawk! cawk! the crew and skipper,
  Are wallowing in the sea:
O what a savoury supper,
  For my old dame and me."

Sir Ralph De Blanc-Minster, of Bien-aimé.

The Vow.

Hush! 'tis a tale of the elder time,
Caught from an old barbaric rhyme;
How the fierce Sir Ralph, of the haughty hand,
Harnessed him for our Saviour's land.

"Time trieth troth," thus the lady said,
"And a warrior must rest in Bertha's bed.
Three years let the severing seas divide,
And strike thou for Christ and thy trusting bride."

So he buckled on the beamy blade,
That Gaspar of Spanish Leon made;
Whose hilted cross is the aweful sign,
It must burn for the Lord and His tarnished shrine.

The Adieu.

"Now a long farewell! tall Stratton Tower,
    Dark Bude! thy fatal sea:
And God thee speed in hall and bower,
    My manor of Bien-aimé.

"Thou, too, farewell my chosen bride,
    Thou Rose of Rou-tor land :
Though all on earth were false beside,
    I trust thy plighted hand.

"Dark seas may swell, and tempests lower,
    And surging billows foam,
The cresset of thy bridal bower,
    Shall guide the wanderer home.

"On! for the cross in Jesu's land,
    When Syrian armies flee :
One thought shall thrill my lifted hand,
    I strike for God and thee."

The Battle.

HARK! how the brattling trumpets blare,
Lo! the red banners flaunt the air;
And see, his good sword girded on,
The stern Sir Ralph to the wars is gone.

Hurrah! for the Syrian dastards flee :
Charge! charge! ye Western chivalry.
Sweet is the strife for God's renown,
The Cross is up, and the Crescent down.

The weary warrior seeks his tent:
For the good Sir Ralph is pale and spent!
Five wounds he reaped in the field of fame:
Five in his blessèd Master's name.

The solemn Leech looks sad and grim,
As he binds and soothes each gory limb;
And the solemn Priest must chant and pray,
Lest the soul unhouseled pass away.

The Treachery.

A sound of horsehoofs on the sand:
And lo! a page from Cornish land:
"Tidings," he said, as he bent the knee,
"Tidings, my lord, from Bien-aimé.

"The owl shrieked thrice from the warder's tower:
The crown-rose withered in her bower:
Thy good gray foal, at evening fed,
Lay in the sunrise stark and dead."

"Dark omens three!" the sick man cried,
"Say on the woe thy looks betide."
"Master! at bold Sir Rupert's call,
Thy Lady Bertha fled the hall."

The Scroll.

"Bring me," he said, "that scribe of fame,
Symeon el Siddekah his name:
With parchment skin, and pen in hand,
I would devise my Cornish land.

"Seven goodly manors, fair and wide,
Stretch from the sea to Tamar side:
And Bien-aimé, my hall and bower,
Nestles beneath tall Stratton Tower.

"All these I render to my God,
By seal and signet, knife and sod:
I give and grant to Church and poor,
In franc-almoign for evermore.

"Choose ye seven men among the just,
And bid them hold my lands in trust;
On Michael's morn, and Mary's day,
To deal the dole, and watch and pray.

"Then bear me coldly o'er the deep,
'Mid my own people I would sleep:
Their hearts shall melt, their prayers will breathe,
Where he who loved them rests beneath.

"Mould me in stone as here I lie,
My face upturned to Syria's sky:
Carve ye this good sword at my side,
And write the legend, 'True and tried.'

"Let mass be said, and requiem sung:
And that sweet chime I loved be rung;
Those sounds along the northern wall,
Shall thrill me like a trumpet-call."

Thus said he—and at set of sun,
The bold Crusader's race was run.
Seek ye his ruined hall and bower?
Then stand beneath tall Stratton Tower.

The Mort-Main.

Now the Demon had watched for the warrior's soul,
'Mid the din of war where blood-streams roll;
He had waited long on the dabbled sand,
Ere the Priest had cleansed the gory hand.

Then as he heard the stately dole,
Wherewith Sir Ralph had soothed his soul;
The unclean spirit turned away,
With a baffled glare of grim dismay.

But when he caught those words of trust,
That sevenfold choice among the just,
"Ho! ho!" cried the fiend with a mock at heaven,
"I have lost but one, I shall win my seven."

Mawgan of Melhuach [b].

I.

'Twas a fierce night when old Mawgan died,
Men shuddered to hear the rolling tide:
The wreckers fled fast from the aweful shore,
They had heard strange voices amid the roar.

II.

"Out with the boat there," some one cried,—
"Will he never come? we shall lose the tide:
His berth is trim and his cabin stored,
He's a weary long time coming on board."

III.

The old man struggled upon the bed:
He knew the words that the voices said;
Wildly he shrieked as his eyes grew dim,
"He was dead! he was dead! when I buried him."

[b] Published in "Once a Week."

IV.

Hark yet again to the devilish roar,
" He was nimbler once with a ship on shore ;
Come! come! old man, 'tis a vain delay,
We must make the offing by break of day."

V.

Hard was the struggle, but at the last,
With a stormy pang old Mawgan passed,
And away, away, beneath their sight,
Gleamed the red sail at pitch of night.

Modryb Marya—Aunt Mary.

A CHRISTMAS CHANT.

IN old and simple-hearted Cornwall, the household names "Uncle" and "Aunt" were uttered and used as they are to this day in many countries of the East, not only as phrases of kindred, but as words of kindly greeting and tender respect. It was in the spirit therefore of this touching and graphic usage, that they were wont on the Tamar side to call the Mother of God in their loyal language *Modryb Marya*, or Aunt Mary.

Now of all the trees by the king's highway,
    Which do you love the best?
O! the one that is green upon Christmas Day,
    The bush with the bleeding breast.
Now the holly with her drops of blood for me:
For that is our dear Aunt Mary's tree.

Its leaves are sweet with our Saviour's Name,
    'Tis a plant that loves the poor:
Summer and winter it shines the same,
    Beside the cottage door.
O! the holly with her drops of blood for me:
For that is our kind Aunt Mary's tree.

'Tis a bush that the birds will never leave :
    They sing in it all day long ;
But sweetest of all upon Christmas Eve,
    Is to hear the robin's song.
'Tis the merriest sound upon earth and sea :
For it comes from our own Aunt Mary's tree.

So of all that grow by the king's highway,
    I love that tree the best ;
'Tis a bower for the birds upon Christmas Day,
    The bush of the bleeding breast.
O ! the holly with her drops of blood for me :
For that is our sweet Aunt Mary's tree.

The Doom-Well of St. Madron.

I.

"Plunge thy right hand in St. Madron's spring,
If true to its troth be the palm you bring:
But if a false sigil thy fingers bear,
Lay them the rather on the burning share."

II.

Loud laughed King Arthur when-as he heard
That solemn friar his boding word:
And blithely he sware as a king he may,
"We tryst for St. Madron's at break of day."

III.

"Now horse and hattock, both but and ben,"
Was the cry at Lauds, with Dundagel men;
And forth they pricked upon Routorr side,
As goodly a raid as a king could ride.

IV.

Proud Gwennivar rode like a queen of the land,
With page and with squire at her bridle hand;
And the twice six knights of the stony ring,
They girded and guarded their Cornish king.

V.

Then they halted their steeds at St. Madron's cell:
And they stood by the monk of the cloistered well;
"Now off with your gauntlets," King Arthur he cried,
"And glory or shame for our Tamar side."

VI.

'Twere sooth to sing how Sir Gauvain smiled,
When he grasped the waters so soft and mild;
How Sir Lancelot dashed the glistening spray
O'er the rugged beard of the rough Sir Kay.

VII.

Sir Bevis he touched and he found no fear:
'Twas a beniteé stoup to Sir Belvidere;
How the fountain flashed o'er King Arthur's Queen,
Say, Cornish dames, for ye guess the scene.

VIII.

"Now rede me my riddle, Sir Mordred, I pray,
My kinsmen, mine ancient, my Bien-aimé;
Now rede me my riddle, and rede it aright,
Art thou traitorous knave or my trusty knight?"

IX.

He plunged his right arm in the judgment well,
It bubbled and boiled like a cauldron of hell:
He drew and he lifted his quivering limb,
Ha! Sir Judas, how Madron had sodden him.

X.

Now let Uter Pendragon do what he can,
Still the Tamar river will run as it ran:
Let king or let kaisar be fond or be fell,
Ye may harowe their troth in St. Madron's well.

A Christ-Cross Rhyme.

I.

Christ His Cross shall be my speed,
Teach me, Father John, to read:
That in church on holy day,
I may chant the psalm and pray.

II.

Let me learn, that I may know
What the shining windows show:
Where the lovely Lady stands,
With that bright Child in her hands.

III.

Teach me letters, A, B, C,
Till that I shall able be,
Signs to know and words to frame,
And to spell sweet Jesus' Name.

IV.

Then, dear master, will I look,
Day and night in that fair book,
Where the tales of saints are told,
With their pictures, all in gold.

V.

Teach me, Father John, to say,
Vesper-verse and matin-lay:
So when I to God shall plead,
Christ His Cross shall be my speed.

The Mystic Magi.

I.

Three ancient men in Bethlehem's cave,
   With aweful wonder stand :
A voice had called them from their grave,
   In some far Eastern land.

II.

They lived : they trod the former earth,
   When the old waters swelled,
The Ark, that womb of second birth,
   Their house and lineage held.

III.

Pale Japhet bows the knee with gold,
   Bright Sem sweet incense brings,
And Cham the myrrh his fingers hold :
   Lo ! the three orient kings.

IV.

Types of the total earth, they hailed
   The signal's starry frame :
Shuddering with second life, they quailed
   At the Child Jesu's Name.

V.

Then slow the Patriarchs turned and trod,
   And this their parting sigh:
"Our eyes have seen the living God,
   And now—once more to die."

NOTE.

THE SOUTHERN CROSS.

It is chronicled in an old Armenian myth, that the Wise Men of the East were none other than the three sons of Noe, and that they were raised from the dead to represent, and to do homage for all mankind, in the cave of Bethlehem. Other legends are also told: one, that these patriarch princes of the flood did not ever die, but were rapt away alive into Enoch's paradise, and were then re-called to begin the solemn gesture of world-wide worship to the King-born Child. Another saying holds, that when their days were full, these Arkite fathers fell asleep, and were laid at rest in a cavern of Ararat, until Messias was born, and that then an angel aroused them from the slumber of ages to bow down and to hail as the heralds of many nations, the awful Child. Be this as it may, whether the Mystic Magi were Sem, Cham, and Japhet, in their first or second existence, under their own names, or those of other men; or whether they were three long-descended and royal sages from the loins or the land of Balaam; one thing has been delivered for very record, that supernatural shape of clustering orbs, which was embodied suddenly from surrounding light, and framed to be the beacon of their westward way, *was and is* the Southern Cross. It was not a solitary signal-fire, but a miraculous constellation: a pentacle of stars whereof two shone for the Transome, and three for the Stock, and which went above and before the travellers day and night radiantly, until it came and stood over where the young Child lay. And then! what then? must these faithful orbs dissolve and die? shall the gleaming trophy fall? Nay—not so. When it had fulfilled the piety of its first-born office, it arose, and amid the vassalage of every stellar and material law, it moved onward and on, obedient to the impulse of God the Trinity, journeying evermore towards the South, until that starry image arrived in the predestined sphere of future and perpetual abode: to bend, as to this day it bends, above the peaceful sea, in everlasting memorial of the Child Jesus: The Southern Cross.

The Cell.

I.

How wildly sweet, by Hartland Tower,
  The thrilling voice of prayer :
A seraph, from his cloudy bower,
  Might lean to listen there.

II.

For time and place, and storied days,
  To that gray fane have given,
Hues that might win an angel's gaze,
  'Mid scenery of heaven.

III.

Above, the ocean breezes sweep,
  With footsteps firm and free :
Around, the mountains guard the deep,
  Beneath, the wide wide sea.

IV.

Enter! the arching roofs expand,
  Like vessels on the shore ;
Inverted, when the fisher-band
  Might tread their planks no more.

V.

But reared on high in that stern form,
    Lest faithless hearts forget
The men that braved the ancient storm,
    And hauled the early net.

VI.

The tracery of a quaint old time,
    Still weaves the chancel screen:
And tombs, with many a broken rhyme,
    Suit well this simple scene.

VII.

A Saxon font, with baptism bright,
    The womb of mystic birth:
An altar, where, in angels' sight,
    Their Lord descends to earth.

VIII.

Here glides the spirit of the psalm,
    Here breathes the soul of prayer:
The aweful Church—so hushed—so calm,
    Ah! surely God is there.

IX.

And lives no legend on the wall?
    No theme of former men?
A shape to rise at fancy's call,
    And sink in graves again?

X.

Yes! there, through yonder portal stone,
    With whispered words they tell,
How once the monk, with name unknown,
    Prepared that silent cell.

XI.

He came with griefs that shunned the light,
    With vows long breathed in vain:
Those arches heard, at dead of night,
    The lash, the shriek, the pain;—

XII.

The prayer that rose and fell in tears,
    The sob, the bursting sigh:
Till woke with agony of years,
    The exceeding bitter cry.

XIII.

This lasted long—as life will wear,
    E'en though in anguish nursed—
Few think what human hearts can bear,
    Before their sinews burst.

XIV.

It lasted long—but not for aye :
    The hour of freedom came :
In that dim niche the stranger lay,
    A cold and silent frame.

XV.

What sorrows shook the strong man's soul,
    What guilt was rankling there,
We know not—time may not unrol
    The page of his despair.

XVI.

He sleeps in yonder nameless ground,
    A cross hath marked the stone :
Pray ye, his soul in death hath found,
    The peace to life unknown.

XVII.

And if ye mourn that man of tears,
    Take heed, lest ye too fall;
A day may mar the rest, that years
    Shall seek but not recal.

XVIII.

Nor think that deserts soothe despair,
    Or shame in cells is screened;
For Thought, the demon, will be there,
    And Memory, the fiend.

XIX.

Then waft, ye winds, this tale of fear,
    Breathe it in hall and bower,
Till reckless hearts grow hushed to hear,
    The Monk of Hartland Tower.

The Lost Ship: "The President."

She sailed from New York for England on the 11th of March, 1841, and was never heard of more.

I.

SPEAK! for thou hast a voice, perpetual sea!
   Lift up thy surges with some signal word:
Shew where the pilgrims of the waters be,
   For whom a nation's thrilling heart is stirred.

II.

They went down to thy waves with joyous pride,
   They trod with stedfast feet thy billowy way:
The eyes of wondering men beheld them glide
   Swift in the arrowy distance—where are they?

III.

Didst thou arise upon that giant frame?
   Mad, that the strength of man with thee should strive:
And proud, thy rival element to tame,
   Didst swallow them in conscious depths, alive?

IV.

Or, shorn and powerless, hast thou bade them lie,
    Their stately ship, a carcase of the foam:
Where still they watch the ocean and the sky,
    And fondly dream that they have yet a home?

V.

If thou hast drawn them, mighty tide, declare,
    To some far-off immeasurable plain,
'Mid all things wild and wonderful, and where
    The magnet woos her iron mate in vain.

VI.

Doth hope still soothe their souls, or gladness thrill?
    Is peace amid those wanderers of the foam?
Say, is the old affection yearning still,
    With all the blessèd memories of home?

VII.

Or, is it over? Life, and breath, and thought,
    The living feature, and the breathing form.
Is the strong man become a thing of nought,
    And the red blood of rank no longer warm?

VIII.

Thou answerest not—thou stern and haughty sea;
    There is no sound in earth, or wave, or air:
Roll on, ye tears! O what shall solace be
    To hearts that pant for hope, but breathe despair?

IX.

Nay, mourner! there is sunlight o'er the deep,
    A gentle rainbow on the darkling cloud:
A voice more mighty than the storms shall sweep
    The shore of tempests when the storm is loud.

X.

What though they woke the whirlwinds of the West,
    Or roused the tempest from some Eastern lair?
Or clave the cloud with thunder in its breast?
    Lord of the aweful waters! Thou wert there.

XI.

All-Merciful! the day, the doom were Thine:
    Thou didst surround them on the seething sea,
Thy love too deep, Thy mercy too divine
    To quench them in an hour unmeet for Thee.

XII.

If winds were mighty, Thou wert in the gale;
   If their feet failed them, in Thy midst they trod;
Storms could not urge the bark, or force the sail,
   Or rend the quivering helm—away from God.

The Poor Man and his Parish Church.
A TRUE TALE.

I.

The poor have hands, and feet, and eyes,
    Flesh, and a feeling mind:
They breathe the breath of mortal sighs,
    They are of human kind.
They weep such tears as others shed,
    And now and then they smile:—
For sweet to them is that poor bread,
    They win with honest toil.

II.

The poor men have their wedding-day:
    And children climb their knee:
They have not many friends, for they
    Are in such misery.
They sell their youth, their skill, their pains,
    For hire in hill and glen:
The very blood within their veins,
    It flows for other men.

III.

They should have roofs to call their own,
    When they grow old and bent:
Meek houses built of dark gray stone,
    Worn labour's monument.
There should they dwell, beneath the thatch,
    With threshold calm and free:
No stranger's hand should lift the latch,
    To mark their poverty.

IV.

Fast by the church those walls should stand,
    Her aisles in youth they trod:—
They have no home in all the land,
    Like that old House of God.
There, there, the Sacrament was shed,
    That gave them heavenly birth;
And lifted up the poor man's head
    With princes of the earth.

V.

There in the chancel's voice of praise,
    Their simple vows were pour'd;
And angels looked with equal gaze
    On Lazarus and his Lord.

There, too, at last, they calmly sleep,
    Where hallowed blossoms bloom ;
And eyes as fond and faithful weep,
    As o'er the rich man's tomb.

VI.

They told me of an ancient home,
    Beside a churchyard wall,
Where roses round the porch would roam,
    And gentle jasmines fall :
There dwelt an old man, worn and blind,
    Poor, and of lowliest birth ;
He seemed the last of all his kind,—
    He had no friend on earth.

VII.

Men saw him till his eyes grew dim,
    At morn and evening tide
Pass, 'mid the graves, with tottering limb
    To the gray chancel's side :
There knelt he down, and meekly prayed
    The prayer his youth had known ;
Words by the old Apostles made,
    In tongues of ancient tone.

VIII.

At Matin-time, at evening hour,
    He bent with reverent knee:
The dial carved upon the tower,
    Was not more true than he.
This lasted till the blindness fell
    In shadows round his bed;
And on those walls he loved so well,
    He looked and they were fled.

IX.

Then would he watch, and fondly turn,
    If feet of men were there,
To tell them how his soul would yearn,
    For the old place of prayer:
And some would lead him on, to stand,
    While fast their tears would fall,
Until he felt beneath his hand
    The long-accustomed wall.

X.

Then joy in those dim eyes would melt,
    Faith found the former tone;
His heart within his bosom felt
    The touch of every stone.

He died—he slept beneath the dew,
    In his own grassy mound:
The corpse, within the coffin, knew
    That calm, that holy ground.

XI.

I know not why—but when they tell
    Of houses fair and wide,
Where troops of poor men go to dwell
    In chambers side by side:—
I dream of that old cottage door,
    With garlands overgrown,
And wish the children of the poor
    Had flowers to call their own.

XII.

And when they vaunt, that in those walls
    They have their worship day,
Where the stern signal coldly calls
    The prisoned poor to pray,—
I think upon that ancient home,
    Beside the churchyard wall,
Where roses round the porch would roam,
    And gentle jasmines fall.

XIII.

I see the old man of my lay,
   His gray head bowed and bare:
He kneels by one dear wall to pray,
   The sunlight in his hair.
Well! they may strive, as wise men will,
   To work with wit and gold;
I think my own dear Cornwall still,
   Was happier of old.

XIV.

O! for the poor man's church again,
   With one roof over all;
Where the true hearts of Cornish men,
   Might beat beside the wall:
The altars where, in holier days,
   Our fathers were forgiven;
Who went with meek and faithful ways,
   Through the old aisles to heaven.

Morwenna Statio.

The Stow, or the place, of St. Morwenna; hence the *Breviate, hodie,* Morwenstow.

I.

My Saxon shrine! the only ground,
    Wherein this weary heart hath rest:
What years the birds of God have found,
    Along thy walls their sacred nest:
The storm—the blast—the tempest shock,
    Have beat upon those walls in vain;
She stands—a daughter of the rock—
    The changeless God's eternal fane.

II.

Firm was their faith, the ancient bands,
    The wise of heart in wood and stone;
Who reared with stern and trusting hands,
    These dark gray towers of days unknown:
They filled these aisles with many a thought,
    They bade each nook some truth reveal;
The pillared arch its legend brought,
    A doctrine came with roof and wall.

III.

Huge, mighty, massive, hard, and strong,
    Were the choice stones they lifted then :
The vision of their hope was long,
    They knew their God, those faithful men.
They pitched no tent for change or death,
    No home to last man's shadowy day;
There! there! the everlasting breath,
    Would breathe whole centuries away.

IV.

See now, along that pillared aisle
    The graven arches, firm and fair :
They bend their shoulders to the toil,
    And lift the hollow roof in air.
A sign! beneath the ship we stand,
    The inverted vessel's arching side;
Forsaken—when the fisher-band
    Went forth to sweep a mightier tide.

V.

Pace we the ground! our footsteps tread,
    A cross—the builder's holiest form :
That awful couch, where once was shed
    The blood, with man's forgiveness warm.

And here, just where His mighty breast,
    Throbbed the last agony away ;
They bade the voice of worship rest,
    And white-robed Levites pause and pray.

VI.

Mark ! the rich rose of Sharon's bowers,
    Curves in the paten's mystic mould :
The lily, lady of the flowers
    Her shape must yonder chalice hold.
Types of the mother and the son,
    The twain in this dim chancel stand :
The badge of Norman banners, one,
    And one a crest of English land.

VII.

How all things glow with life and thought,
    Where'er our faithful fathers trod !
The very ground with speech is fraught,
    The air is eloquent of God.
In vain would doubt or mockery hide
    The buried echoes of the past ;
A voice of strength, a voice of pride,
    Here dwells amid the storm and blast.

VIII.

Still points the tower, and pleads the bell,
    The solemn arches breathe in stone :
Window and wall have lips to tell,
    The mighty faith of days unknown.
Yea, flood and breeze, and battle-shock,
    Shall beat upon this church in vain ;
She stands, a daughter of the rock,
    The changeless God's eternal fane.

The Tamar Spring.

The source of this storied river of the West is on a rushy knoll, in a moorland of this parish. The Torridge also flows from the self-same mound.

I.

Fount of a rushing river! wild flowers wreathe
   The home where thy first waters sunlight claim:
The lark sits hushed beside thee, while I breathe,
   Sweet Tamar spring! the music of thy name.

II.

On! through thy goodly channel, on! to the sea!
   Pass amid heathery vale, tall rock, fair bough:
But never more with footstep pure and free,
   Or face so meek with happiness as now.

III.

Fair is the future scenery of thy days,
   Thy course domestic, and thy paths of pride:
Depths that give back the soft-eyed violets gaze,
   Shores where tall navies march to meet the tide.

IV.

Thine, leafy Tetcott, and those neighbouring walls,
  Noble Northumberland's embowered domain;
Thine, Cartha Martha, Morwell's rocky falls,
  Storied Cotehele, and Ocean's loveliest plain.

V.

Yet false the vision, and untrue the dream,
  That lures thee from thy native wilds to stray:
A thousand griefs will mingle with that stream,
  Unnumbered hearts shall sigh those waves away.

VI.

Scenes fierce with men, thy seaward current laves,
  Harsh multitudes will throng thy gentle brink;
Back with the grieving concourse of thy waves,
  Home to the waters of thy childhood shrink.

VII.

Thou heedest not! thy dream is of the shore,
  Thy heart is quick with life; on! to the sea!
How will the voice of thy far streams implore,
  Again amid these peaceful weeds to be!

VIII.

My soul! my soul! a happier choice be thine,
    Thine the hushed valley, and the lonely sod;
False dream, far vision, hollow hope resign,
    Fast by our Tamar Spring, alone with God!

The Child Jesus.

A CORNISH CAROL.

I.

WELCOME that Star in Judah's sky,
   That voice o'er Bethlehem's palmy glen :
The lamp, far sages hailed on high,
   The tones that thrilled the shepherd men :
Glory to God in loftiest heaven !
   Thus angels smote the echoing chord ;
Glad tidings unto man forgiven,
   Peace from the presence of the Lord.

II.

The shepherds sought that birth divine,
   The Wise Men traced their guided way ;
There, by strange light and mystic sign,
   The God they came to worship lay.
A human Babe in beauty smiled,
   Where lowing oxen round Him trod :
A maiden clasped her aweful Child,
   Pure offspring of the breath of God.

III.

Those voices from on high are mute,
    The Star the Wise Men saw is dim:
But hope still guides the wanderer's foot,
    And faith renews the angel hymn:
Glory to God in loftiest heaven!
    Touch with glad hand the ancient chord;
Good tidings unto man forgiven,
    Peace from the presence of the Lord.

The Song of the School: St. Mark's, Morwenstow.

I.

Sing to the Lord the children's hymn,
    His gentle love declare,
Who bends amid the seraphim,
    To hear the children's prayer.

II.

He! at a mother's breast was fed,
    Though God's own Son was He;
He learnt the first small words He said,
    At a meek mother's knee.

III.

He held us to His mighty breast,
    The children of the earth;
He lifted up His hands and blessed
    The babes of human birth.

IV.

So shall He be to us our God,
    Our gracious Saviour too:
The scenes we tread, His footsteps trod,
    The paths of youth He knew.

V.

Lo! from the stars His face will turn,
    On us with glances mild:
The angels of His presence yearn
    To bless the little Child.

VI.

Keep us, O Jesu Lord, for Thee,
    That so, by Thy dear grace,
We, children of the font, may see
    Our heavenly Father's face.

VII.

Sing to the Lord the children's hymn,
    His tender love declare,
Who bends amid the seraphim,
    To hear the children's prayer.

The Dirge.

I.

"Sing from the chamber to the grave!"
   Thus did the dead man say:
"A sound of melody I crave,
   Upon my burial-day.

II.

"Bring forth some tuneful instrument,
   And let your voices rise:
My spirit listened, as it went,
   To music of the skies.

III.

"Sing sweetly while you travel on,
   And keep the funeral slow:—
The angels sing where I am gone,
   And you should sing below.

IV.

"Sing from the threshold to the porch!
   Until you hear the bell:
And sing you loudly in the church,
   The Psalms I love so well.

V.

"Then bear me gently to my grave,
    And as you pass along,
Remember 'twas my wish to have
    A pleasant funeral song.

VI.

"So earth to earth, and dust to dust!
    And though my flesh decay,
My soul shall sing among the just,
    Until the judgment day."

NOTE.

The first line of these verses haunted the memory and the lips of a good and blameless young farmer who died in my parish some years ago. It was, as I conceive, a fragment of some forgotten dirge, of which he could remember no more. But it was his strong desire that "the words" should be "put upon his headstone," and he wished me also to write "some other words, to make it complete." I fulfilled his entreaty, and the stranger who visits my churchyard will find this dirge carven in stone, "in sweet remembrance of the just," and to the praise of the dead, Richard Cann.

The Storm.

I.

War, 'mid the ocean and the land!
The battle-field, Morwenna's strand,
Where rock and ridge the bulwark keep,
The giant-warders of the deep.

II.

They come! and shall they not prevail,
The seething surge, the gathering gale?
They fling their wild flag to the breeze,
The banner of a thousand seas.

III.

They come—they mount—they charge in vain,
Thus far, incalculable main!
No more! thine hosts have not o'erthrown,
The lichen on the barrier stone.

IV.

Have the rocks faith, that thus they stand,
Unmoved, a grim and stately band,
And look, like warriors tried and brave,
Stern, silent, reckless, o'er the wave?

V.

Have the proud billows thought and life,
To feel the glory of the strife?
And trust, one day, in battle bold,
To win the foeman's haughty hold?

VI.

Mark where they writhe with pride and shame,
Fierce valour, and the zeal of fame!
Hear how their din of madness raves,
The baffled army of the waves!

VII.

Thy way, O God, is in the sea,
Thy paths, where aweful waters be:
Thy Spirit thrills the conscious stone,
O Lord, Thy footsteps are not known!

The Figure-head of the Caledonia at Her Captain's Grave.

I.

We laid them in their lowly rest,
    The strangers of a distant shore;
We smoothed the green turf on their breast,
    'Mid baffled Ocean's angry roar;
And there, the relique of the storm,
We fixed fair Scotland's figured form.

II.

She watches by her bold, her brave,
    Her shield towards the fatal sea:
Their cherished lady of the wave,
    Is guardian of their memory.
Stern is her look, but calm, for there
No gale can rend or billow bear.

III.

Stand, silent image! stately stand,
   Where sighs shall breathe and tears be shed,
And many a heart of Cornish land,
   Will soften for the stranger dead.
They came in paths of storm—they found,
This quiet home in Christian ground.

Genoveva.

PART THE FIRST.

Morning.

I.

Now hearken, lords and ladies gay,
    And ye shall understand
The wonders of a legend-lay,
    From the old German land!
She, of my song, in Eden's bowers,
    A sainted lady lies;
And wears a chaplet of the flowers
    That grow in Paradise.

II.

Her father gloried in her birth,
    That daughter of his fame;
The sweetest sound he knew on earth
    Was Genoveva's name.

She dwelt, a fair and holy child,
    Beside her mother's knee :
She grew, a maiden meek and mild,
    And pure as pure could be.

III.

And so it was, that when the maid
    Fulfilled her childhood's vow,
Saint Hildorf's lifted hands were laid
    Upon no lovelier brow.
And said they, as along the aisle
    The lords and ladies poured,
" How will she gladden with her smile
    The castle of her lord !"

IV.

Right soon a stately champion came,
    For that bright damsel's hand ;
The sound of County Siegfried's fame
    Was sung in many a land.
He came, he knelt, he wooed, he won,
    As warriors win, the bride ;
Duke Pfalz hath hailed him as his son,
    At Genoveva's side.

V.

Then might you hear the matin-bell,
    With echoes low and sweet;
Where at St. Hildorf's sacred cell
    The youth and maiden meet.
And hark! they plight the mystic vow,
    The troth that time shall try,
When years have worn the beamy brow,
    And quenched the laughing eye.

VI.

Now turn we to the castle gate,
    Wreathed with the peaceful vine,
Where County Siegfried holds his state,
    Beside the Rhine! the Rhine!
They bring white blossoms from the bowers,
    The rose-leaves hide the ground;
Ah! gentle dame, beneath the flowers,
    The coiling worm is found!

VII.

Yet day by day went bounding on,
    Nor would the warrior roam:
The brightness of his lady shone,
    Throughout Lord Siegfried's home.

She was the garland of his days,
    His blessing and his fame:
His happy hearth hath won the praise
    Of Genoveva's name.

VIII.

But hark! that stern and sudden sound,
    Along the castle wall:
It shook the echo from the ground,
    That startling trumpet-call.
"To arms! To horse! The Moor! The Moor!
    His pagan banners fly:
The Spaniard and the Frank implore
    Thy German chivalry."

IX.

Then might you see, at break of day,
    The stately Siegfried stand:
Harnessed, and in his old array,
    His good sword in his hand.
"And fare-thee-well!" the soldier said,
    "My lady bright and dear:"
He spake, and bent his haughty head,
    To hide a warrior's tear.

X.

" Farewell! and thou my castellain,
    My liege-man true and tried,
Shield, till thy lord shall turn again,
    My lady and my bride.
And ye, good saints, with unseen eyes,
    Watch her in solemn care :
An angel well might leave the skies,
    At Genoveva's prayer."

PART THE SECOND.

Evening.

I.

Ah! woe is me! and well-a-day!
    What scenes of sorrow rise:
And hark! the music of my lay
    Must breathe the breath of sighs.
That guardian,—he of vaunted fame,
    He seeks a deed abhorred:
He woos to sorrow and to shame,
    The lady of his lord.

II.

But she, fair Genoveva, stands,
   A pure and peerless bride;
Her angel lifts his sheltering hands,
   For ever at her side.
She kneels, she breathes some simple verse,
   Taught by her mother's care;
And the good saints in heaven rehearse,
   The gentle lady's prayer.

III.

Yet strife and anguish lasted long,
   Till he—that fiendish man,
The anger of his sin was strong,
   And thus his fury ran:—
" Bind ye this foul and wanton dame,
   False to my master's bed:
Hide in the earth both sin and shame,
   Her blood be on her head."

IV.

They took the stern command he gave,
   Two vassals fierce and rude;
They bare her to a nameless grave,
   Far in a distant wood.

There knelt she down and meekly prayed,
   In language soft and mild:
" I bear beneath my breast," she said,
   " Your lord, Count Siegfried's child.

V.

" Then let me tarry but awhile,
   Far, far, from earthly eye,
That I may see my infant smile,
   And lay me down and die.
Nay, spare me, in sweet Mary's name,
   Who stood by Jesu's cross:
He from a mother's bosom came,
   That He might die for us."

VI.

They melted at the voice they heard,
   They left her lonely there:
The holy angels helped her word,
   There is such force in prayer.
Then wandered she, where that wild wood,
   A tangled pathway gave,
Till, lo! in secret solitude,
   A deep and mossy cave.

VII.

A source of quiet waters shone,
    Along a shadowy glade;
And branches, fair to look upon,
    A dreamy shelter gave.
Her eyes are closed—but not to sleep;
    She bends—but not to pray:
Thrilled with the woes that mothers weep,
    The lonely lady lay.

VIII.

She sees—what is it nestling near?
    A soft fair form is nigh:
She hears—sweet Lord, what doth she hear?
    A low and infant cry.
It is her son! her son! the child,
    The firstborn of her vow:
See, in his face his father smiled,
    He bears Lord Siegfried's brow.

IX.

Good angels! 'twas a sight to see,
    That cavern dark and wild:—
The nameless stream—the silent tree,
    The mother and her child.

And hark! he weeps—that voice of tears
    Proclaims a child of earth;
O, what shall soothe for holier years,
    The sorrow of his birth!

X.

There was no font, no sacred shrine,
    No servant of the Lord:
The waters of the mystic sign,
    A mother's hand hath poured.
She breathed on him a word of woes,
    His life in tears begun:
The name a Hebrew mother chose,
    Ben-oni—Sorrow's son.

XI.

But ah! what miseries betide
    A mother and her pains!
Her child must die, for famine dried
    The fountain of her veins.
She saw the anguish of his face,
    She heard his bitter cry,
And went forth from that woeful place,
    She could not see him die.

XII.

Yet still, again, her feet must turn
    Back to that cavern wild:
Yea! even in death, she fain would yearn
    Once more upon her child.
What doth she see? a fair young doe
    A mother's task hath done,
Bent at his side: her milk must flow
    To soothe the lady's son.

XIII.

She wept,—she wept, she could no less,
    Tears sweet and grateful ran;
The mute thing of the wilderness
    Hath softer heart than man.
She came, that wild deer of the herd,
    Moved by some strange control;
There was a mystic touch that stirred
    The yearnings of her soul.

XIV.

And there they dwelt, the gentle three,—
    In peace, if not in joy,
Until he stood beside her knee,
    A fair and thoughtful boy.

The doe, the lady, and the youth,
    Seven long and weary years,
Their calm and patient life; in sooth
    It was a sight for tears.

XV.

She fed him with the forest fruits,
    That summer branches gave;
She gathered wild and wholesome roots,
    To cheer their wintry cave:
They drank from that fair fountain's bed,
    Whose faithful waters run,
Bright as when first his name they shed,
    Ben-oni—Sorrow's son.

XVI.

And she hath framed, with chosen boughs,
    A simple cross of wood;
And taught the lad his childhood's vows,
    To Jesu, mild and good.
He learnt the legend of the Cross,
    How Mary's blessèd Son
Came down from heaven to die for us,
    And peace and pardon won.

XVII.

He heard that shadowy angels roam
    Along the woodland dell,
To lead the blessèd to a home
    Where saints and martyrs dwell.
So, when the lady wept and prayed,
    He soothed her secret sighs:
"Sweet mother, let us die," he said,
    "And rest in Paradise."

XVIII.

"Alas! my son, my tender son,
    What wilt thou do," she sighed,
"When I thy mother shall be gone?—
    Thou hast no friend beside.
There is thy Sire of Heavenly birth,
    His love is strong and sure:
But he, thy father of the earth,
    He spurns thee from his door."

XIX.

"Nay, tell me, mother dear," he said,
    "I pray thee tell to me,
Are they not, all men, gone and dead,
    Except thy son and thee?"

"Ah! no, there be, my gentle child,
    Whole multitudes afar;
Yet is it happier in this wild,
    Than where their dwellings are.

XX.

"They cast me out to woe and shame,
    Here in this den to hide:
They blighted Genoveva's name,
    Lord Siegfried's chosen bride.
But soon the weary will have rest,
    I breathe with failing breath:
There is within thy mother's breast,
    The bitterness of death."

XXI.

"Then, mother kind, in thy dark grave.
    Alone, thou shalt not lie:
Before our Cross, here in this grave,
    Together let us die.
Yea, let me look on no man's face,
    Since such stern hearts there be:
But here, in this our lonely place,
    Here will I die with thee."

XXII.

"Ah! noble heart! thy words are sooth,
    I breathe their sound again:
Better to pass away in youth,
    Than live with bearded men."
And thou! the Lady of his birth,
    Farewell! a calm farewell!
Thou wert not meant for this vile earth,
    But with the saints to dwell.

PART THE THIRD.

Another Day.

I.

Mark ye, how spear and helmet glare,
    And red-cross banners shine,
While thrilling trumpets cleave the air
    Along the Rhine! the Rhine!
Count Siegfried from the wars is come,
    And gathering vassals wait,
To welcome the stern warrior home
    To his own castle gate.

II.

But where is she, his joy, his pride,
    The garland of his fame?
Away! away! her image hide,
    He cannot brook her name.
Yet soon the whispered words are breathed,
    And faithful lips declare,
How a vile serpent's folds were wreathed
    Around their lady fair.

III.

They tell his vassal's treacherous crime,
    The bow his malice bent,
Till Genoveva, in her prime,
    Had perished, innocent.
Alas! what torrent tears must roll
    In fierce and angry shower!
O! what shall soothe Count Siegfried's soul
    In that o'erwhelming hour?

IV.

He hides him in some vaulted room,
    Far from the light of day;
He will not look on beauty's bloom,
    Nor hear the minstrel's lay.

They try him with the trumpet sound
    On many an echoing morn;
They tempt him forth with hawk and hound,
    And breathe the hunter's horn.

V.

They loose the gazehound from the chain,
    They bring forth steed and spear,
Lord Siegfried's hand must rule the rein,
    And rouse the ruddy deer.
On! through the wild, the war-horse bounds
    Beneath his stately form,
He charges 'mid those rushing hounds
    With footsteps like the storm.

VI.

"Down! Donner, down! hold, Hubert, hold!
    What is yon sight of fear?
A strange wild youth, a maiden bold,
    That guard yon panting deer!
A fleecy skin was folded round
    Her breast, with woman's pride,
And some dead fawn the youth hath found,
    He wears its dappled hide.

VII.

"Who? whence are ye?" the warrior said,
　"That haunt this secret cave?
Ha! is it so? and do the dead
　Come from their hollow grave?"
"I live, I breathe the breath of life,
　No evil have I done;
I am thy true, thy chosen wife,
　And this is Siegfried's son!"

VIII.

He stood, as severed souls may stand
　At first, when forth they fare,
And shadowy forms—a stranger-band
　Will greet them in the air.
He bounds, he binds her to his heart,
　His own, his rescued bride:
No more, O never more to part,
　E'en death shall not divide.

IX.

See now, they move along the wild,
　With solemn feet and slow,
The warrior and his graceful child,
　The lady and the doe.

They stand before the castle gate,
    Rich with the clustering vine,
Again shall Siegfried hold his state,
    Beside the Rhine! the Rhine!

X.

They come, they haste from many a land,
    For fast the tidings spread,
And there doth Genoveva stand,
    Bright as the arisen dead.
Her mother weeps, by God's dear grace
    Glad tears are in her eye;
Duke Pfalz hath seen his daughter's face,
    And now—now let him die.

XI.

Yea, from his calm and distant cell
    The sainted Hildorf came,
His spirit bowed beneath the spell
    Of Genoveva's name.
He came, he sought that solemn cave,
    The lady's patient home,
He measured it with aisle and nave,
    He shaped a shadowy dome.

XII.

He knelt in votive solitude,
   He fixed both saint and sign,
And bade them build, in that lone wood,
   A fair and stately shrine.
There might you read for many an age,
   In the rich window's ray,
Traced, as along some pictured page,
   The legend of my lay.

XIII.

The image of their youth was there,
   The bridegroom and the bride;
The porch, where Genoveva fair
   Knelt at her Siegfried's side.
There, through the storied glass, the scene
   In molten beauty falls,
When she, with mild and matron mien,
   Shone in her husband's halls.

XIV.

There was the cave, the wood, the stream,
   In radiance soft and warm,
And evermore the noon-day beam
   Came through some angel's form.

The youth was shewn, in that wild dress,
    His mother's cross he bare;
Saint John in the old wilderness
    Was not more strangely fair.

XV.

But where they breathe their holiest vows,
    And eastern sunbeams fall,
A simple cross, of woodland boughs,
    Stands by the chancel wall.
It is the lady's lonely sign,
    By mournful fingers made,
The self-same symbol decks the shrine
    That soothed the cavern's shade.

XVI.

Behind yon altar, reared on high,
    A lady breathes in stone;
A sculptured deer is crouching nigh,
    An infant weeps alone.
A word is there, but not of woe,
    One voice, a prayer to claim,
Beneath the lady and the doe
    Is Genoveva's name.

XVII.

Thus lived, thus loved she, and she died,
    But old, and full of days;
Ask ye how time and truth have tried
    The legend of her praise?
She of my song, in Eden's bowers
    A sainted lady lies,
And wears a garland of the flowers
    That grow in Paradise.

The Token Stream of Tidna Combe.

I.

A SOURCE of gentle waters, mute and mild,
   A few calm reeds around the sedgy brink,
The loneliest bird, that flees to waste or wild,
   Might fold its feathers here in peace to drink.

II.

I do remember me of such a scene,
   Far in the depths of memory's glimmering hour,
When earth looked e'en on me with tranquil mien,
   And life gushed, like this fountain in her bower.

III.

But lo! a little on, a gliding stream,
   Fed with fresh rills from fields before unknown,
Where the glad roses on its banks may dream
   That watery mirror spreads for them alone.

IV.

Ah! woe is me! that flood, those flowers, recal
   A gleaming glimpse of Time's departed shore,
Where now no dews descend, no sunbeams fall,
   And leaf and blossom burst, no more, no more!

V.

See now! with heart more stern, and statelier force,
    Through Tidna's vale the river leaps along;
The strength of many trees shall guard its course,
    Birds in the branches soothe it with their song.

VI.

O type of a far scene! the lovely land!
    Where youth wins many a friend, and I had one:
Still do thy bulwarks, dear old Oxford, stand?
    Yet, Isis, do thy thoughtful waters run?

VII.

But hush! a spell is o'er thy conscious wave;
    Pause and move onward with obedient tread;
At yonder wheel they bind thee for their slave;
    Hireling of man, they use thy toil for bread.

VIII.

Still is thy stream an image of the days
    At duty's loneliest labour meekly bound;
The foot of joy is hushed, the voice of praise:
    We twain have reached the stern and anxious ground.

IX.

And now what hills shall smile, what depths remain,
    Thou tamed and chastened wanderer, for thee?
A rocky path, a solitary plain,
    Must be thy broken channel to the sea.

X.

Come then, sad river, let our footsteps blend
    Onward, by silent bank, and nameless stone:
Our years began alike, so let them end,—
    We live with many men, we die alone.

XI.

Why dost thou slowly wind and sadly turn,
    As loth to leave e'en this most joyless shore?
Doth thy heart fail thee? do thy waters yearn
    For the far fields of memory once more?

XII.

Ah me! my soul, and thou art treacherous too,
    Linked to this fatal flesh, a fettered thrall:
The sin, the sorrow, why would'st thou renew?
    The past, the perished, vain and idle all!

XIII.

Away ! behold at last the torrent leap,
  Glad, glad to mingle with yon foamy brine ;
Free and unmourned, the cataract cleaves the
    steep—
  O river of the rocks, thy fate is mine !

Aishah Schechinah.

I.

A SHAPE, like folded light, embodied air,
   Yet wreathed with flesh, and warm;
All that of heaven is feminine and fair,
   Moulded in visible form.

II.

She stood, the Lady Schĕchĭnăh of earth,
   A chancel for the sky;
Where woke, to breath and beauty, God's own birth,
   For men to see Him by.

III.

Round her, too pure to mingle with the day,
   Light, that was life, abode;
Folded within her fibres meekly lay
   The link of boundless God.

IV.

So linked, so blent, that when, with pulse fulfilled,
   Moved but that infant hand,
Far, far away, His conscious Godhead thrilled,
   And stars might understand.

V.

Lo, where they pause, with intergathering rest,
    The Threefold, and the One;
And lo, He binds them to her orient breast,
    His manhood girded on.

VI.

The zone, where two glad worlds for ever meet,
    Beneath that bosom ran:
Deep in that womb the conquering Paraclete
    Smote Godhead on to man.

VII.

Sole scene among the stars, where, yearning, glide
    The Threefold and the One;
Her God upon her lap, the Virgin bride,
    Her awful Child, her Son!

NOTE.

AISHAH.

THIS was the happy name of Eve in the days of her innocence. When she stood before Adam in her blameless beauty, he said, being inspired, "She shall be called Aishah," that is to say, man's, or man's own, because she is taken out of Aish, 'man.' It was afterwards, when she had shuddered into sin, that the man called the name of his wife Eve. Now the household word for the sinless Mother in the cottage of Nazareth, and on the lips of her Son, was also Aishah; it was in memory of the former phrase of Eden, a sound of mingled endearment and respect. It was not, in that native language, as it is in our own mean and meagre speech, a mere appellative of sex, 'woman,' but Aishah, the tender and the graphic title of the twain: the bride of the garden, man's own, all innocent: and of Mary, maiden-Mother of God. So at Cana, and on Calvary, Jesus made chosen utterance of that only name, Aishah. At the marriage, when, with her woman's zeal for the honour of the feast, the Mother made haste to her Son, and said, suddenly, "They have no wine," Jesus answered, and with the long-accustomed smile, "What have *we*, Aishah?" He said in the exact letter, "What is to Me, and to thee, Aishah?" He signified, with a very usual idiom, "What have I, and what hast thou, Aishah?" He meant in the spirit of His voice and smile, "What have we *not*, Aishah? Are not all things under our feet? Mine hour, the hour that thou wottest of, is not yet come; but still"—and the well-known look of Nazareth and home revealed the rest. So she turned to the servants, and said, "Whatsoever He shall say unto you, do."

SCHECHINAH.

THIS, the cloudy signal of the Presence, is the most majestic symbol of Our Lady throughout the oracles. The sacramental element of the Schechinah, which I have named Numyne, was called by the Rabbins, "Mater et Filia Dei," and was always a feminine noun. They say it was a stately pillar, or column of soft and fleecy cloud, which took ever and anon, as to Elias upon Carmel, the outline of a human shape or form, "Vestigium hominis." Within its breast sojourned the glory of the Presence, as in a tent. Therefore I claim, with all reverence, the right to use the title Aishah Schechinah. The sound of this latter word is a dactyle.

The Lady's Well.

I.

It flowed, like light, from the voice of God,
    Silent, and calm, and fair;
It shone where the child and the parent trod,
    In the soft and evening air.

II.

"Look at that spring, my father dear,
    Where the white blossoms fell:
Why is it always bright and clear?
    And why the Lady's Well?"

III.

"Once on a time, my own sweet child,
    There dwelt across the sea
A lovely mother, meek and mild,
    From blame and blemish free.

IV.

"And Mary was her blessèd name,
    In every land adored:
Its very sound deep love should claim
    From all who love their Lord.

V.

"A Child was hers—a heavenly birth,
    As pure as pure could be:
He had no father of the earth,
    The Son of God was He.

VI.

"He came down to her from above,
    He died upon the Cross:
We never can do for Him, my love,
    What He hath done for us.

VII.

"And so to make His praise endure,
    Because of Jesu's fame,
Our fathers called things bright and pure
    By His fair mother's name.

VIII.

"She is the Lady of the Well,—
　Her memory was meant,
With lily and with rose, to dwell
　By waters innocent."

A Ballad for a Cottage Wall.

I.

A CHILD sate by the meadow-gate,
    A tender girl and young;
With many a tear her eyes were wet,
    And thus she sate and sung:—

II.

"Ah! woe is me! for I have no grace,
    Nor goodness as I ought:
I never shall go to the happy place,
    And 'tis all my parents' fault.

III.

"To this bad world they brought me in,
    A place where all must grieve;
With flesh of misery and sin,
    From Adam and from Eve.

IV.

"And then they shunned the churchyard path,
    Where holy angels haunt:
They would not bear their child of wrath
    To yonder blessed font.

V.

"They kept me from that second birth,
    Which God to baptism gave;
And now I have no hope on earth,
    Nor peace beyond the grave.

VI.

"Yet a thought is in my mind to-day,—
    It came I know not how;
I will go to the font at church, and say
    I seek my baptism now.

VII.

"Yes! God is kind: I shall then have grace,
    And goodness as I ought;
For oh! if I lose the happy place
    'Twill be my poor parents' fault."

VIII.

'Twas a child of meek and gentle kind,
   A tender girl and young;
And angels put into her mind
   The solemn words she sung.

"By the Waters."

I.

Weep ye not for the dead! they sleep
In hallowed slumbers, calm and deep;
Their bed, the country of their birth,
The dust around them, Hebrew earth.

II.

They cease, and yet bemoan them not;
Their tombs are in the blessèd spot
Where hearth, and home, and altar stand,
With Aaron's shrines, and Judah's land.

III.

But weep ye sore for us! we go
Where rivers of the stranger flow;
And Gentile winds must bear along
The Lord's, the God of Jacob's song.

IV.

We travel to the graves unknown,
To die in cities not our own;
False feet our sepulchres will tread
A breathing nation of the dead.

V.

Bel's loathsome land, and Nebo's sky,—
Our flesh will shudder where we lie;
Bone to his bone will cleave and creep
From the vile earth around our sleep.

VI.

But they, the dead by Jordan's stream,
They hear those waters where they dream;
The floods that fall by Abraham's cave,
And Rachel's tomb, and Isaac's grave.

VII.

Then mourn ye not for them, their sleep
Is pure and blessèd, calm and deep:
But grieve, yea, grieve for us, we go
Where rivers of the stranger flow.

VIII.

No more! no more! O never more,
The hills, the trees, the ocean shore;
Ah! Salem, Gilead, Lebanon,
The Lord, the Lord your God, is gone.

The Vine.

Hearken! there is in old Morwenna's shrine
   A lonely sanctuary of the Saxon days,
   Reared by the Severn sea for prayer and praise,
Amid the carved work of the roof, a vine;
   Its root is where the eastern sunbeams fall,
   First in the chancel, then along the wall;
Slowly it travels on, a leafy line,
   With here and there a cluster, and anon
   More and more grapes, until the growth hath gone
Through arch and aisle. Hearken! and heed the sign.
   See at the altar side the stedfast root,
   Mark well the branches, count the summer fruit:
So let a meek and faithful heart be thine,
And gather from that tree a parable divine.

The Twain.

Two sunny children wandered, hand in hand,
   By the blue waves of far Gennesaret,
   For there their Syrian father drew the net,
With multitudes of fishes, to the land.
   One was the twin, even he whose blessèd name
   Hath in ten thousand shrines this day a fame,—
Thomas the Apostle, one of the ethereal band.
   But he, his Hebrew brother, who can trace
   His name, the city where he dwelt, his place,
Or grave? We know not, none may understand.
   There were two brethren in the field: the one
   Shall have no memory underneath the sun;
The other shines, beacon of many a strand,
A star upon the brow of night, here in the rocky land.

The Well of St. John.[*]

They dreamed not in old Hebron, when the sound
   Went through the city, that the promised son
   Was born to Zachary, and his name was John;
They little thought, that here in this far ground,
   Beside the Severn sea, that Hebrew child
   Would be a cherished memory of the wild;
Here, where the pulses of the ocean bound
   Whole centuries away, while one meek cell,
   Built by the fathers o'er a lonely well,
Still breathes the Baptist's sweet remembrance round.
   A spring of silent waters with his name,
   That from the angel's voice in music came,
Here in the wilderness so faithful found,
It freshens to this day the Levite's grassy mound.

       [*] On Morwenstow Glebe.

The Wolf.

Long centuries agone,—this very day
   In a far wilderness of Syrian sand,
   Urging his steed amid an armèd band,
The wolf of Benjamin was on the prey.
   But lo! a light, a voice, a thrilling sound,
   And where was Saul of Tarsus? sternly bound
A fettered thrall, in darkness there he lay!
   Shall he arise and conquer? can he toil
   Once more in war and yet divide the spoil?
For thus dim Jacob traced the wanderer's way:
   Answer, proud Corinth! stern and stately Rome,
   Soft Ephesus, and thou, the populous home
Of many a city, old Galatia, say,—
Did not the warrior win and wear a conqueror's
      array?

The Saintly Names.

SISTERS were they, the fair and holy twain,
    Marveena and Morwenna; and the vales
    And mountains of their birth were in wild Wales,—
Thence came they in their youth across the main.
    King Breachan was their sire, and his sweet wife
    Gladwise their mother gave them love and life;
Virgins they lived and died—O not in vain!
    One meekly built a solitary cell,
    Where still her lingering memory loves to dwell,
In the old arches of Gray Marham's fane;
    The other sought the sea: her pleasant place
    The pilgrim of the waters still may trace,
Where rock and headland watch the ocean plain.
    Mark how their blended names in music flow,
    The Church of Marham, and Morwenna's Stowe!
Nor let the dreamer of the past complain:
The saints, the sanctuaries, the creed, this very day
    remain. ·

Clovelly.

I.

'Tis eve! 'tis glimmering eve! how fair the scene
    Touched by the soft hues of the dreamy west!
Dim hills afar, and happy vales between,
    With the tall corn's deep furrow calmly blest:
Beneath, the sea! by Eve's fond gale caressed,
    'Mid groves of living green that fringe its side;
Dark sails that gleam on ocean's heaving breast
    From the glad fisher-barks that homeward glide,
    To make Clovelly's shores at pleasant evening-tide.

II.

Hearken! the mingling sounds of earth and sea,
    The pastoral music of the bleating flock,
Blent with the seabird's uncouth melody,
    The waves' deep murmur to the unheeding rock;
And ever and anon the impatient shock
    Of some strong billow on the sounding shore:
And hark! the rowers' deep and well-known stroke,
    Glad hearts are there, and joyful hands once more
    Furrow the whitening wave with their returning oar.

III.

But turn where art with votive hand hath twined
    A living wreath for nature's grateful brow,
Where the lone wanderer's raptured footsteps wind
    'Mid rock, and glancing stream, and shadowy
        bough ;
Where scarce the valley's leafy depths allow
    The intruding sunbeam in their shade to dwell,
There doth the seamaid breathe her human vow,—
    So village maidens in their envy tell—
        Won from her dark blue home by that alluring dell.

IV.

A softer beauty floats along the sky,
    The moonbeam dwells upon the voiceless wave ;
Far off, the night-winds steal away and die,
    Or sleep in music in their ocean cave :
Tall oaks, whose strength the giant-storm might brave,
    Bend in rude fondness o'er the silvery sea ;
Nor can yon mountain raun forbear to lave
    Her blushing clusters where the waters be,
        Murmuring around her home such touching melody.

V.

Thou, quaint Clovelly! in thy shades of rest,
    When timid spring her pleasant task hath sped,
Or summer pours from her redundant breast
    All fruits and flowers along thy valley's bed:
Yes! and when autumn's golden glories spread,
    Till we forget near winter's withering rage,
What fairer path shall woo the wanderer's tread,
    Soothe wearied hope and worn regret assuage?
    Lo! for firm youth a bower, a home for lapsing age.

Ephpheta.

I.

High matins now in bower and hall!
It is the Baptist's festival:
What showers of gold the sunbeams rain,
Through the tall window's purple pane!
What rich hues on the pavement lie,
A molten rainbow from the sky!

II.

But light and shadow loveliest fall
Yonder, along the southward wall,
Where ceased e'en now the chanted hymn
Of that gray man whose eyes are dim:
'Twas an old legend, quaintly sung,
Caught from some far barbaric tongue.

III.

He asks,—and bread of wheat they bring;
He thirsts for water from the spring
Which flowed of old, and still flows on,
With name and memory of Saint John:
So fares the pilgrim in that hall,
E'en on the Baptist's festival.

IV.

"How sad a sight is blind old age!"
Thus said the lady's youthful page:
"He eats, but sees not on that bread
What glorious radiance there is shed;
He drinks from out that chalice fair,
Nor marks the sunlight glancing there."

V.

"Watch! gentle Ronald, watch and pray,
And hear once more an old man's lay:
I cannot see the morning poured,
Ruddy and rich on this gay board;
I may not trace the noonday light,
Wherewith my bread and bowl are bright:—

VI.

"But thou, whose words are sooth, hast said,
That brightness falls on this fair bread;
Thou sayest—and thy tones are true—
This cup is tinged with heaven's own hue:
I trust thy voice; I know from thee
That which I cannot hear nor see.

VII.

"Watch! gentle Ronald, watch and pray!
It is the Baptist's holy day!
Go, where in old Morwenna's shrine
They break the bread and bless the wine;
There meekly bend thy trusting knee,
And touch what sight can never see.

VIII.

"Thou wilt behold, thy lips may share
All that the cup and paten bear;
But life unseen moves o'er that bread,
A glory on that wine is shed;
A light comes down to breathe and be,
Though hid, like summer suns, from me.

IX.

"Watch! gentle Ronald, watch and pray!
Day oft is night and night is day:
The arrowy glance of lady fair
Beholds not things that throng the air;
The clear bright eye of youthful page
Hath duller ken than blind old age."

K

X.

'Tis evensong in bower and hall
On the bold Baptist's festival:
The harp is hushed, and mute the hymn,
The guest is gone whose eyes are dim,
But evermore to Ronald clung
That mystic measure, quaintly sung.

The Signals of Levi.

THE Rabbins have ruled that the daily oblation was never to begin until the Signal of Levi was heard, and the time was thus to be known:—A Levite was placed before cockcrow, on the roof of the Temple, to watch the sky; and when the day had so far dawned that he could see Hebron, a city on the heights where John the Baptizer was afterwards born, then he blew with his trumpet an appointed sound, and the sacrifice began.

SIGNAL THE FIRST.

I.

THERE is light on Hebron now:
   Hark to the trumpet din!
Day dawns on Hebron's brow,
   Let the sacrifice begin.

II.

Hear ye the gathering sound!
   How the lute and harp rejoice,
'Mid the roar of oxen bound,
   And the lamb's beseeching voice.

III.

This day both prince and priest
    Will hold at Salem's shrine
A high and haughty feast
    Of flesh and the ruddy wine.

IV.

For a perilous hour is fled,
    And the fear is vain at last,
Though foretold by sages dead,
    And sworn by the Prophets past.

V.

They said that a mortal birth,
    E'en now would a name unfold,
That should rule the wide, wide earth,
    And quench the thrones of old.

VI.

But no sound, nor voice, nor word,
    The tale of travail brings;
Not an infant-cry is heard
    In the palaces of kings.

VII.

Blossom and branch are bare
   On Jesse's stately stem:
So they bid swart Edom wear
   Fallen Israel's diadem.

VIII.

How they throng the cloistered ground
   'Mid Judah's shame and sin:
Hark to the trumpet-sound!
   Let the sacrifice begin.

SIGNAL THE SECOND.

I.

THERE is light on Hebron's towers,
   Day dawns o'er Jordan's stream,
And it floats where Bethlehem's bowers
   Of the blessèd morning dream.

II.

Yet it wakes no kingly halls,
   It cleaves no purple room;
The soft, calm radiance falls
   On a cavern's vaulted gloom.

III.

But there, where the oxen rest
    When the weary day is done,
How that maiden-mother's breast
    Thrills with her aweful Son!

IV.

A cave, where the fatlings roam,
    By the ruddy heifer trod,
Yea! the mountain's rifted home
    Is the birthplace of a God!

V.

This is He! the mystic birth
    By the sign and voice foretold;
He shall rule the wide, wide earth,
    And quench the thrones of old.

VI.

The Child of Judah's line,
    The Son of Abraham's fame:
Arise, ye lands! and shine
    With the blessèd Jesu's name.

VII.

This is the promised dawn:
    So fades the night of sin;
Lo! the gloom of death is gone,
    Let the sacrifice begin.

SIGNAL THE THIRD.

I.

"Ho! watchman! what of the night?
    Tell, Christian soldier, tell:
Are Hebron's towers in sight?
    Hast thou watched and warded well?"

II.

"Yea! we have paced the wall
    Till the day-star's glimmering birth;
And we breathed our trumpet-call
    When the sunlight walked the earth."

III.

"What sawest thou with the dawn?
    Say, Christian warder, say;
When the mists of night were gone,
    And the hills grew soft with day?"

IV.

"We beheld the morning swell
  Bright o'er the eastern sea;
Till the rushing sunbeams fell
  Where the westward waters be.

V.

"City and bulwark lay
  Rich with the orient blaze,
And rocks, at the touch of day,
  Gave out a sound of praise.

VI.

"No hill remained in cloud,
  There lurked no darkling glen;
And the voice of God was loud
  Upon every tongue of men.

VII.

"There shall never more be night
  With this eternal sun;
There be Hebrons many in sight,
  And the sacrifice is done!"

The Sea-bird's Cry.

I.

'Tis harsh to hear, from ledge or peak,
The sunny cormorant's tuneless shriek;
Fierce songs they chant, in pool or cave,
Dark wanderers of the western wave.
Here would the listening landsman pray
For memory's music, far away;
Soft throats that nestling by the rose,
Soothe the glad rivulet as it flows.

II.

Cease, stranger! cease that fruitless word,
Give eve's hushed bough to woodland bird:
Let the winged minstrel's valley-note,
'Mid flowers and fragrance, pause and float.
Here must the echoing beak prevail,
To pierce the storm, and cleave the gale;
To call, when warring tides shall foam,
The fledgling of the waters home.

III.

Wild things are here of sea and land,
Stern surges and a haughty strand;
Sea-monsters haunt yon caverned lair,
The mermaid wrings her briny hair;
That cry, those sullen accents sound
Like native echoes of the ground.
Lo! He did all things well who gave
The sea-bird's voice to such a wave.

The Burial Hour.

I.

"At eve should be the time," they said,
" To close their brother's narrow bed:"
'Tis at that pleasant hour of day
The labourer treads his homeward way.

II.

His work was o'er, his toil was done,
And therefore, with the set of sun,
To wait the wages of the dead
We laid our hireling in his bed.

The First Prince of Wales.

I.

"Weep, noble lady, weep no more,
    The woman's joy is won:
Fear not! thy time of grief is o'er,
    And thou hast borne a son."

II.

Then ceased the Queen from pain and cry,
    And as she sweetly smiled,
The tears stood still within her eye,
    The mother saw her child.

III.

"Now bear him to the castle-gate;"
    Thus did the King command:
There, stern and stately all, they wait
    The warriors of the land.

IV.

They met—another lord to claim,-
    And loud their voices rung,—
"We will not brook the stranger's name,
    Nor serve a Saxon tongue.

V.

"Our king shall breathe a British birth,
    And speak with native voice;
He shall be famous in the earth,
    The chieftain of our choice."

VI.

Then might you hear the drawbridge fall,
    And echoing footsteps nigh:
And hearken! by yon haughty wall
    A low and infant cry.

VII.

"God save your Prince!" King Edward said,
    "Your wayward wish is won:
Behold him from his mother's bed,
    My child—my firstborn son.

VIII.

"Here in his own, his native place,
    His future feet shall stand,
And rule the children of your race
    In language of the land."

IX.

'Twas strange to see; so sternly smiled
    Those warriors gray and grim:
How little thought King Edward's child
    Who thus would welcome him!

X.

Nor knew they then how proud the tone
    They taught their native vales;
The sound whole nations lived to own,—
    "God save the Prince of Wales!"

The Death-Race.

I.

Watch ye, and ward ye! a ship in sight,
And bearing down for Trebarra Height,
She folds her wings by that rocky strand:
Watch ye, and ward ye! a boat on land!

II.

Hush! for they glide from yonder cave
To greet these strangers of the wave;
Wait! since they pace the seaward glen
With the measured tread of mourning men.

III.

"Hold! masters, hold! ye tarry here,
What corse is laid on your solemn bier?
Yon minster-ground were a calmer grave
Than the roving bark, or the weedy wave!"

IV.

"Strong vows we made to our sister dead
To hew in fair France her narrow bed;
And her angry ghost will win no rest
If your Cornish earth lie on her breast."

V.

They rend that pall in the glaring light:
By St. Michael of Carne! 'twas an aweful sight!
For those folded hands were meekly laid
On the silent breast of a shrouded maid.

VI.

"God speed, my masters, your mournful way!
Go, bury your dead where best ye may:
But the Norroway barks are over the deep,
So we watch and ward from our guarded steep."

VII.

Who comes with weapon? who comes with steed?
Ye may hear far off their clanking speed;
What knight in steel is thundering on?
Ye may know the voice of the grim Sir John.

VIII.

"Saw ye my daughter, my Gwennah bright,
"Borne out for dead at the deep of night?"
"Too late! too late!" cried the warder pale,
"Lo! the full deck, and the rushing sail!"

IX.

They have roused that maid from her trance of
 sleep,
They have spread their sails to the roaring deep;
Watch ye and ward ye! with wind and tide,
Fitz-Walter hath won his Cornish bride.

The Comet of 1861.

"Terroresque de cœlo et signa magna." S. Luc. xxi. 11.

I.

Whence art thou, sudden comet of the sun?
    In what far depths of God thine orient place?
Whence hath thy world of light such radiance won
    To gleam and curve along the cone of space?

II.

Why comest thou, weird wanderer of the air?
    What is thine oracle for shuddering eyes?
Wilt thou some myth of crownless kings declare,
    Scathed by thy fatal banner of the skies?

III.

Or dost thou glide, a seething orb of doom,
    Bristling with penal fires, and thick with souls;
The severed ghosts that throng thy peopled womb,
    Whom Azrael, warder of the dead, controls?

IV.

Throne of some lost archangel, dost thou glare,
    After long battle, on that conquering height?
Vaunt of a victory that is still despair,
    A trophied horror on the arch of night?

V.

But lo! another dream: thou starry god,
    Art thou the mystic seedsman of the sky?
To shed new worlds along thy radiant road,
    That flow in floods of billowy hair on high?

VI.

Roll on! yet not almighty: in thy wrath
    Thou bendest like a vassal to his king;
Thou darest not o'erstep thy graven path,
    Nor yet one wanton smile of brightness fling.

VII.

Slave of a mighty Master! be thy brow
    A parable of night, in radiance poured:
Amid thy haughtiest courses, what art thou?
    A lamp to lead some pathway of the Lord!

NOTE.

"THE CONE OF SPACE."

SPACE is that measured part of God's presence which is inhabited by the planets and the sun. The boundary of space is the outline of a cone, and the pathway of every planet is one of the sections of that figured form.

Absalom's Pillar.

I.

Rear yonder rock ! vast, pillared, and alone,
Like some grim god revealed in aweful stone ;
There build my place, and bid my memory stand,
Throned in mid air, to rule along the land.

II.

There hew my name where Judah's daughters glide
To weave their shadowy dance at evening-tide ;
Lo ! their soft voices thrill the stony shade,—
" Here the Prince Absalom, who died in youth, is laid."

III.

I have no son, no daughter of my fame
To breathe, 'mid future hearts, their father's name ;
I live with many men, I die alone ;
I go into the ground : rear the surviving stone !

The Ringers of Lancells Tower.

THESE ancient men rang at the accession of George the Third, and all again at his jubilee. Three of them lived on to ring in George the Fourth; and two survived to celebrate, in their native tower, the coronation of King William the Fourth.

I.

THEY meet once more! that ancient band,
With furrowed cheek and failing hand;
One peal to-day they fain would ring,
The jubilee of England's king!

II.

They meet once more! but where are now
The sinewy arm, the laughing brow,
The strength that hailed, in happier times,
King George the Third with lusty chimes?

III.

Yet proudly gaze on that lone tower,
No goodlier sight hath hall or bower;
Meekly they strive—and closing day
Gilds with soft light their locks of gray.

IV.

Hark! proudly hark! with that true tone
They welcomed him to land and throne;
So ere they die they fain would ring
The jubilee of England's king.

V.

Hearts of old Cornwall, fare ye well!
Fast fade such scenes from field and dell;
How wilt thou lack, my own dear land,
Those trusty arms, that faithful band!

Featherstone's Doom.

I.

Twist thou and twine! in light and gloom
   A spell is on thine hand;
The wind shall be thy changeful loom,
   Thy web, the shifting sand.

II.

Twine from this hour, in ceaseless toil,
   On Blackrock's sullen shore;
Till cordage of the sand shall coil
   Where crested surges roar.

III.

'Tis for that hour, when, from the wave,
   Near voices wildly cried;
When thy stern hand no succour gave,
   The cable at thy side.

IV.

Twist thou and twine! in light and gloom
 The spell is on thine hand;
The wind shall be thy changeful loom,
 Thy web, the shifting sand.

NOTE.

THE Blackrock is a bold, dark, pillared mass of schist, which rises midway on the shore of Widemouth Bay, near Bude, and is held to be the lair of the troubled spirit of Featherstone the wrecker, imprisoned therein until he shall have accomplished his doom.

Trebarrow.

I.

Did the wild blast of battle sound,
Of old, from yonder lonely mound?
Race of Pendragen! did ye pour,
On this dear earth, your votive gore?

II.

Did stern swords cleave along this plain
The loose rank of the roving Dane?
Or Norman chargers' sounding tread
Smite the meek daisy's Saxon head?

III.

The wayward winds no answer breathe,
No legend cometh from beneath,
Of chief, with good sword at his side,
Or Druid in his tomb of pride.

IV.

One quiet bird, that comes to make
Her lone nest in the scanty brake;
A nameless flower, a silent fern—
Lo! the dim stranger's storied urn.

V.

Hark! on the cold wings of the blast
The future answereth to the past;
The bird, the flower, may gather still,
Thy voice shall cease upon the hill!

NOTE.

THE word *tre* signifies in the ancient Cornish tongue 'the place of abode,' and *barrow* means 'a burial mound.' The word "Trebarrow" implies, therefore, 'a dwelling among the graves;' and my house at North Tamerton was so named by me because it was surrounded by these green heaps of the dead. Some of these I opened, and in the centre of one of them I found an urn of baked clay filled with human ashes, and a patera, which I still possess, of the same material. It denotes in all likelihood the entombment of a Keltic priest, and that of pre-Christian times.

Sophie Granville Thynne, on her Fifth Birthday.

I.

With all that earth hath holy, and all that heaven hath blest,
We hail thy native morning, fairy princess of the West!
For thy father's blood is thrilling in the daughter of his race,
And thy mother's eyes are drooping in thy soft and gentle face.

II.

'Tis well those eyes were kindled where the sunset floods the plains,
For the western life of Granville is bounding in thy veins;
As a queen upon the dais shall thy future footsteps stand,
Thou shalt rule our Tamar side, a born lady of the land.

III.

Like a brook alive with gladness shall thy happy
    girlhood flow
Where the heavens come down to rest, on the storied
    hills of Stowe;
And the billowy laugh of waters along thy native
    shore
Shall chant thy bridal morning with the sea's ex-
    ulting roar.

IV.

Ay! the children yet unborn shall arise and learn
    to trace
The old ancestral features how they haunt thy
    matron-face;
For the self-same smile shall beam upon thine own,
    thy chosen knight,
That wooed the proud Sir Beville home from Stam-
    ford's gory fight.

V.

Lady Grace once more shall waken in her fair and
    happy prime:
God shield thee from such tears as fell at Lans-
    downe's fatal time;

She will glide, and she will gleam again, her children at her knee,
For her innocence and loveliness were prophecies of thee.

VI.

So now, my gentle Sophie, I have sung this native song
To pray in votive numbers for thy happy years and long;
Till thy father's ancient line shall revive beneath thy breast,
And thy mother's living eyes on thine own sweet babe shall rest.

VII.

I hear thy days resounding, as they roll in gladness on,
'Mid other bards that greet thee, when I am hushed and gone:
For loftier tones shall waken, and happier voices flow,
To teach thy children's children the glories of old Stowe.

The Lady's Offering.

I.

A web of woven wool, fringed all around,
   Ruddy and rich in hue, like Syrian wine;
With golden leaves inlaid on that dark ground,
   That seemed just shed from some o'ershadowing
      vine:
   Such was the lady's offering at Morwenna's shrine.

II.

We laid it on the altar, while the word
   Lingered in echoes o'er the unconscious wall;
The voice that prophesied our God had heard
   The sound of alms, and would remember all;
   'Twas the Child Jesu's day, the Bethlehem festival.

III.

We offered it to Him:—scorn not the phrase
   Ye proud and stately magnates of the land;
Grudge not the poor their pence, nor God His praise,
   Though as our simple fathers stood, we stand,
   And render thus our gifts with meek and votive
      hand.

IV.

We left it in that chancel decked with flowers,
  And boughs that blossomed like old Aaron's rod;
For faithful hands had built them leafy bowers
    Along our aisles, such as the angels trod
      When Moses saw the bush and Abraham talked
        with God.

"Pater vester pascit illa."

Our bark is on the waters! wide around
    The wandering wave; above, the lonely sky.
    Hush! a young sea-bird floats, and that quick cry
Shrieks to the levelled weapon's echoing sound,
Grasp its lank wing, and on, with reckless bound!
    Yet, creature of the surf, a sheltering breast
    To-night shall haunt in vain thy far-off nest,
A call unanswered search the rocky ground.
    Lord of leviathan! when Ocean heard
Thy gathering voice, and sought his native breeze;
When whales first plunged with life, and the proud deep
Felt unborn tempests heave in troubled sleep;
    Thou didst provide, e'en for this nameless bird,
Home, and a natural love, amid the surging seas!

"Lord, whither goest Thou?"

(From the German.)

I.

BLOOD flowed throughout the stately city,
   The cruel Cæsar's haughty home;
Men perished, and there was no pity,
   Nor rescue, in imperial Rome.
It was when Nero's wrath was sorest,
   And death and sorrow marked his way,
When, like the wild beast of the forest,
   He revelled o'er his quivering prey.

II.

Then Christian limbs were bowed and blended,
   Prostrate where peopled pathways meet;
Coated with slime, till pain was ended
   By the slow march of trampling feet;
Or smeared around with pitch for burning,
   Their fires along the pavement spread,
Torches to light the crowds, returning
   From some fierce game where Christians bled.

III.

Now blessèd blood that day was sweeter
    Than the red stream of lowlier gore;
So shall the veins of good Saint Peter
    Slake the fierce Gentiles' thirst once more.
His guilt, that he the blind and cripple
    Had touched, until they saw and trod;
His crime, that hosts of Roman people
    Sought at his voice the Christian's God.

IV.

Then fastly came the woeful warning,
    Where the meek Church had met to sigh;
The place, the doom, the fatal morning
    When Simon, Jonah's son, shall die.
So many a loving accent pleaded,—
    " Baffle wild Nero's wrath, and flee:
Thine arm, thy living voice, are needed
    The succour of God's Church to be."

V.

Their secret wish his own resembled,
    Forth from the gate his footsteps fare:
Whom did he see, that thus he trembled?
    O! blessèd Jesu! Thou wert there.

"Now whither goest Thou, dear Master?"
　　The Apostle said, with kindling eye:—
"Once more to brook the old disaster,
　　Again upon My Cross to die.

VI.

"To die for those who would have perished
　　Had they been left to love like thine;
The flock thou oughtest to have cherished,
　　The lambs and sheep so dearly Mine."
Thus said the Lord, and forthwith vanished,
　　Even as He did in days of yore;
And he, the Apostle, turned and banished
　　The fear of death for evermore.

To Eva Valentine,

On her Sixth Birthday, May 16, 1864.

I.

Queen of the months! thy starry bloom
Floods with glad hues our Cornish combe;
Thy birds are loud with heaven's own mirth,—
Hast thou no song for Eva's birth?

II.

No tempest woke, no winds were wild,
To greet thy dawn, my gentle child;
But first in summer's loveliest bowers
Thy voice was heard amid the flowers.

III.

So was thy name, the garden bride,
Thrilled at its sound with joy and pride:
Her Eden held one fatal tree,—
Be earth all Paradise to thee!

IV.

Ah, Eva! she, our mother, stood
At once in noon-day womanhood;
In her full eyes there could not shine
The simple witchery of thine.

V.

Yet, 'mid the conscious trees, began
The war that won her vassal, man:
He saw his freedom in the skies,
And lost it for his lady's eyes.

VI.

So thou, when woman's love shall warm
The pulses of thy thrilling form,
Unfold, for one dear thrall to rest,
The paradise of Eva's breast.

To Matilda Valentine,

On her Birthday, July 17, 1864.

I.

MAID of the North! a distant sky
Kindled with light thy large dark eye :
And now within its glances rest
The soft beams of our glowing west.

II.

Welcome that sun! its joyous ray
Smiles on Matilda's native day ;
And, lo! to soothe her path are given
The happiest hues of earth and heaven.

III.

Hail! omen of that dawning time
When Maud shall hear her marriage-chime.
And light and music, blended, greet
The pausing matron's homeward feet.

IV.

Such and so cloudless be the days
Whereon thy noon of life shall gaze ;
So may a cloudless sunset shine,
Maid of the North, for thee and thine.

"Blue Eyes melt, dark Eyes burn[d]."

I.

THE eyes that melt, the eyes that burn,
The lips that make a lover yearn,
These flashed on my bewildered sight.
Like meteors of the northern night.

II.

Then said I in my wild amaze,
"What stars be they that greet my gaze?
Where shall my shivering rudder turn?
To eyes that melt, or eyes that burn?

III.

" Ah! safer far the darkling sea
Than where such perilous signals be;
To rock, and storm, and whirlwind turn
From eyes that melt, and eyes that burn."

[d] From "All the Year Round."

Queen Guennivar's Round.[e]

I.

NAIAD for Grecian waters!
   Nymph for the fountain-side!
But old Cornwall's bounding daughters
   For gray Dundagel's tide.

II.

The wild wind proudly gathers
   Round the ladies of the land;
And the blue wave of their fathers
   Is joyful where they stand.

III.

Naiad for Grecian waters!
   Nymph for the fountain-side!
But old Cornwall's bounding daughters
   For gray Dundagel's tide.

[e] Published in "All the Year Round."

IV.

Yes! when memory rejoices
   In her long-belovèd theme,
Fair forms and thrilling voices
   Will mingle with my dream.

V.

Naiad for Grecian waters!
   Nymph for the fountain-side!
But old Cornwall's bounding daughters
   For gray Dundagel's tide.

King Arthur's Waes-hael.

The Rubric.

WHEN the brown bowl is filled for yule, let the dome or upper half be set on; then let the waes-haelers kneel one by one and draw up the wine with their reeds through the two bosses at the rim. Let one breath only be drawn by each of the morrice for his waes-hael.

I.

WAES-HAEL for knight and dame!
  O! merry be their dole;
Drink-hael! in Jesu's name
  We fill the tawny bowl;
But cover down the curving crest,
Mould of the orient lady's breast.

II.

Waes-hael! yet lift no lid:
  Drain ye the reeds for wine!
Drink-hael! the milk was hid
  That soothed that Babe divine;
Hushed, as this hollow channel flows,
He drew the balsam from the rose.

III.

Waes-hael! thus glowed the breast
    Where a God yearned to cling;
Drink-hael! so Jesu pressed
    Life from its mystic spring;
Then hush, and bend in reverent sign,
And breathe the thrilling reeds for wine.

IV.

Waes-hael! in shadowy scene,
    Lo! Christmas children we;
Drink-hael! behold we lean
    At a far Mother's knee;
To dream, that thus her bosom smiled,
And learn the lip of Bethlehem's Child.

NOTE.

THE rounded shape of the bowl for waes-hael was intended to recal the image of a mother's breast; and thus it was meant, with a touching simplicity, to blend the thought of our Christmas gladness with the earliest nurture of the Child Jesus.

On the Grave of a Child in Morwenstow Churchyard.

Those whom God loves die young;
   They see no evil days;
No falsehood taints their tongue,
   No wickedness their ways.

Baptized—and so made sure
   To win their safe abode;
What could we pray for more?
   They die, and are with God.

The Legend of Saint Cecily.

"Brought an Angel down."

I.

Uprose the morning with a ruddy glow!
    Uprose her gentle forehead, wreathed with day!
The mountain-top—the wood—the river's flow,
    Gleamed softly—and aloud the matin-lay
Of singing birds, their leafy bowers below,
    Swelled into song to greet the Orient ray;
While yet the sun, full-quivered, paused on high,
To launch his arrowy beams along the sky.

II.

Then, at the casement of his chosen bride,
    A young man listened to a sweeter song;
Fair Cecily's—of all her race the pride—
    What eye could greet a lovelier in the throng?
To win her vows how many a knight had sighed,
    With mortal love her virgin life to wrong:
But what was earth with all its golden glare?
Her eyes were heavenward, and her soul was there.

III.

The maiden chants, her Saviour's grace to sing;
    Her harp is mingled with that thrilling sound:
The music trembles on the quivering string,
    Like some sweet sorcery of enchanted ground.
Well might an angel-hand the magic bring,
    That first in sainted Cecily was found,
The spell that bade the aweful organ roll
The storm of music o'er the shuddering soul.

IV.

The youth drew near with glad and blushing brow,
    "It is the day," he said, "the morning beams!
Friends wait with anxious ears our uttered vow,—
    See! on the temple-dome the sunlight gleams!
The wreath, the sacrifice are ready now;
    The multitude along the pathway streams—
Lo! the priests beckon, and the guests are loud,
And the wide gates enfold a gathering crowd."

V.

She lifted up her voice, "What then? shall I,
    The vassal of the Lord, become thy slave?
To live a common life beneath the sky!
    I, that my vows to Jesu-Master gave?

He, the good Shepherd, rules me with His eye,
  My God to follow, and thy wrath to brave!
Would that thou durst at yon true altar stand,
Where I am safe, amid the angel-band."

VI.

Mute with deep sorrow, still he stood, and stern;
  Away! away! a sad and last adieu!
And yet, fond hope, his lingering feet return,
  Once more the sorrow of her eye to view:
He smiled, to hide the love that yet would yearn;
  "Hast thou," he said, "an angel tried and true?
Shew me thy friend! let me but see him shine!
My heart shall bend to thee! thy God be mine."

VII.

"It shall be done!" the unshrinking maiden said,
  "The Lord will yield His trusting handmaid grace;"
The bridegroom went, with slow and mournful tread,
  Once more, at evening-tide, that path to trace.
He came! he saw! O vision fair and dread!
  The maiden at the altar bowed her face;
Her starry eyes were rapt in trusting prayer,
And o'er that brow an angel stood, on air!

VIII.

Death-tokens held that spirit in his hand!
   He laid a rose upon the young man's breast;
The maiden took a lily of the land—
   Those flowers the symbols of a martyr's rest.
Thereby the twain could meekly understand
   That life would fleetly fade and death was best.
Both fell for God! and now in every tongue
Valerien lives, and Cecily is sung.

Saint Thekla.

The First Lily in the Garden of God.

I.

Sweet is the shrinking image of the rose,
    When her first blush is o'er the mossy ground :
Her brow is bent where many a blossom grows :
    She gazes on the flowers that shine around,
Till with the breath of spring her spirit glows,
    And her young branch with lifted leaves is crowned :
Then must her eyes be raised from that low sod,
She bares her breast to heaven and yields her hues
    to God.

II.

Such was the maiden of my lay.   In youth
    She hid her beauty in her father's halls :
He who had wooed her with the words of truth,
    Like moonlight on the snow, his image falls
Upon her vestal spirit :—yet in sooth
    No nobler knight in the high festivals
Of his own city, sought a chosen bride :
He was her father's choice, her own dear mother's
    pride.

III.

Then came Saint Paul the Apostle to those streets;
    Castled Iconium was the city's name:
He came—he taught—how Thekla's bosom beats:
    How his deep language shook her silent frame!
She stood—she listened—till her soul entreats
    The birth of baptism, and its hallowing name.
The words are uttered, and the waters poured,
She breathes the virgin-troth that binds her to the Lord.

IV.

Unheard the bridegroom's voice, and vain his vow,
    In the sweet bondage of the faith to share;
Her high resolves a father may not bow,
    She will not soften at a mother's prayer,
Till with revolted heart and quivering brow,
    The youth will wreak on her his mad despair;
On, to the judgment-seat, with reckless breath,
And there reveals her creed whose doom is angry death.

V.

See! in her city-gate the maiden stands!
    The threat—the promise—all are urged in vain;
She folds upon her breast her faithful hands—
    That calmness in her eye is half-disdain!

She hears the mandate to the soldier-bands,
  "To the wild beasts!" nor will she then complain,
Though Gentile hearts were moved, and many an eye
  Wept to behold her led, all innocent, to die!

VI.

She stood, with gentle and uplifted look,
  When they had loosed the lions on their prey;
But lo! the fierce and famished creatures shook,
  And crouching at her feet, in fondness lay;
There will they rest, though none beside may brook
  Their furious fangs nor soothe their angry way;
"The fire! the flame!" hark, what fierce accents
  rise!
"Yea! scorch her to the gods! there shall be sacrifice."

VII.

A miracle again! another sign!
  The unseen angel of the Lord was there;
They saw the flames, subdued, around her shine,
  And mingle harmless with her waving hair:
And lo! a starry cross, as on a shrine,
  Beamed on the forehead of that maiden fair,
The first bright daughter of the Church, whose fame
Hath won in many a land the martyr's sainted name.

The Quest of the Sangraal.

Ho! for the Sangraal! vanished vase of heaven!
That held, like Christ's own heart, an hin [f] of blood!
Ho! for the Sangraal! . . .
                How the merry shout,
Of reckless riders on the rushing steed,
Smote the loose echo from the drowsy rock
Of grim Dundagel: throned along the sea!

"Unclean! unclean! ten cubits and a span [g],
Keep from the wholesome touch of human-kind:
Stand at the gate, and beat the leper's bell,
But stretch not forth the hand for holy thing,—
Unclean, as Egypt at the ebb of Nile!"

Thus said the Monk: a lean and gnarled man;
His couch was on the rock, by that wild stream
That floods, in cataract, Saint Nectan's Kieve [h]:
One of the choir, whose life is Orison!
They had their lodges in the wilderness,—

  [f] The hin was a Hebrew measure, used for the wine of the sacrifice.
  [g] The distance at which a leper was commanded to keep from every healthy person.
  [h] Or cauldron.

Or built them cells beside the shadowy sea,
And there they dwelt with angels, like a dream:
So they unrolled the volume of the Book,
And filled the fields of the Evangelist
With antique thoughts, that breathed of Paradise!

Uprose they for the quest! the bounding men,
Of the siege perilous, and the granite ring!
They gathered at the rock: yon ruddy tor[i],—
The stony depth where lurked the demon-god,
Till Christ, the mighty Master, drave him forth.

There stood the knights! stately, and stern, and tall;
Tristan; and Percevale; Sir Galahad:
And he, the sad Sir Lancelot of the lay:
Ah me! that logan[k] of the rocky hills,
Pillared in storm, calm in the rush of war,
Shook, at the light touch of his lady's hand!

---

[i] Routor, the red hill, so named from the heath which blossoms on the hill-side.

[k] Logan or shuddering stone. A rock of augury found in all lands, a relic of the patriarchal era of belief. A child or an innocent person could move it, as Pliny records, with a stalk of asphodel, but a strong man, if guilty, could not shake it with all his force.

See! where they move, a battle-shouldering kind!
Massive in mould, but graceful: thorough men:
Built in the mystic measure of the cross:—
Their lifted arms the transome: and their bulk,
The tree, where Jesu, stately stood to die!
Thence came their mastery in the field of war:—
Ha! one might drive battalions, one alone.

See now, they pause;—for in their midst, the King!
Arthur, the son of Uter, and the night:
Helmed with Pendragon; with the crested crown;
And belted with the sheathed excalibur[1],
That gnashed his iron teeth, and yearned for war!
Stern was that look: high natures seldom smile:
And in those pulses beat a thousand kings.
A glance! and they were hushed: a lifted hand,
And his eye ruled them like a throne of light!
Then, with a voice that rang along the moor,
Like the Archangel's trumpet for the dead,—
He spake—while Tamar sounded to the sea.

"Comrades in arms! mates of the table round!
Fair Sirs, my fellows in the bannered ring,—
Ours is a lofty tryst! this day we meet,

[1] A Hebrew name signifying 'champer of the steel.'

Not under shield, with scarf and knightly gage,
To quench our thirst of love in ladies' eyes:
We shall not mount to-day that goodly throne,
The conscious steed, with thunder in his loins,
To launch along the field the arrowy spear :—
Nay, but a holier theme, a mightier quest,—
' Ho! for the Sangraal, vanished vase of God !'

" Ye know that in old days, that yellow Jew,
Accursèd Herod ; and the earth-wide judge,
Pilate the Roman : doomster for all lands—
Or else the Judgment had not been for all,—
Bound Jesu-Master to the world's tall tree,
Slowly to die . . .
    Ha! Sirs, had we been there,
They durst not have assayed their felon deed,—
Excalibur had cleft them to the spine !
Slowly He died, a world in every pang,
Until the hard centurion's cruel spear
Smote His high heart: and from that severed side,
Rushed the red stream that quenched the wrath of
  Heaven !

" Then came Sir Joseph, hight, of Arimathèe,
Bearing that awful vase, the Sangraal !
The vessel of the Pasch, Shere Thursday night:

The selfsame Cup, wherein the faithful Wine
Heard God, and was obedient unto Blood!
Therewith he knelt, and gathered blessèd drops
From his dear Master's Side that sadly fell,
The ruddy dews from the great tree of life:
Sweet Lord! what treasures! like the priceless gems,
Hid in the tawny casket of a king,—
A ransom for an army, one by one!

" That wealth he cherished long; his very soul
Around his ark: bent, as before a shrine!

" He dwelt in orient Syria: God's own land:
The ladder-foot of heaven—where shadowy shapes
In white apparel glided up and down!
His home was like a garner, full of corn
And wine and oil: a granary of God!
Young men, that no one knew, went in and out,
With a far look in their eternal eyes!
All things were strange and rare: the Sangraal
As though it clung to some etherial chain,
Brought down high heaven to earth at Arimathèe.

" He lived long centuries! and prophesied.
A girded pilgrim ever and anon:
Cross-staff in hand, and folded at his side,

The mystic marvel of the feast of blood!
Once, in old time, he stood in this dear land,
Enthralled:—for lo! a sign! his grounded staff
Took root, and branched, and bloomed, like Aaron's
    rod;
Thence came the shrine, the cell; therefore he dwelt,
The vassal of the vase, at Avalon!

"This could not last, for evil days came on,
And evil men: the garbage of their sin
Tainted this land, and all things holy fled.
The Sangraal was not: on a summer eve,
The silence of the sky brake up in sound!
The tree of Joseph glowed with ruddy light:
A harmless fire, curved like a molten vase,
Around the bush, and from the midst, a voice:
Thus hewn by Merlin on a runic stone:—
𝔅𝔦𝔯𝔦𝔬𝔱𝔥: 𝔢𝔩: 𝔖𝔞𝔫𝔫𝔞𝔥: 𝔞𝔲𝔩𝔬𝔥𝔢𝔢: 𝔭𝔢𝔡𝔞𝔥:

"Then said the shuddering seer—he heard and knew
The unutterable words that glide in heaven,
Without a breath or tongue, from soul to soul—

"The land is lonely now: Anathema:
The link that bound it to the silent grasp
Of thrilling worlds is gathered up and gone:

The glory is departed; and the disk
So full of radiance from the touch of God!
This orb is darkened to the distant watch
Of Saturn and his reapers, when they pause,
Amid their sheaves, to count the nightly stars.

"All gone! but not for ever: on a day,
There shall arise a king from Keltic loins,
Of mystic birth and name, tender and true;
His vassals shall be noble, to a man:
Knights strong in battle till the war is won:
Then while the land is hushed on Tamar-side,
So that the warder upon Carradon
Shall hear at once the river and the sea,—
That king shall call a Quest: a kindling cry:
'Ho! for the Sangraal! vanished vase of God!'

"Yea! and it shall be won! a chosen knight
The ninth from Joseph in the line of blood,
Clean as a maid from guile, and fleshly sin,—
He with the shield of Sarras [m]; and the lance,

[m] The city of "Sarras in the spiritual place," is the scene of many a legend of mediæval times. In all likelihood it was identical with Charras or Charran of Holy Writ. There was treasured up the shield, the sure shelter of the Knight of the Quest. The lance which pierced our blessed Saviour's side was also there preserved.

Ruddy and moistened with a freshening stain,
As from a severed wound of yesterday,—
He shall achieve the Graal: he alone!

"Thus wrote Bard Merlin on the Runic hide
Of a slain deer: rolled in an aumry chest.

"And now, fair Sirs! your voices: who will gird
His belt for travel in the perilous ways?
This thing must be fulfilled:—in vain our land
Of noble name, high deed, and famous men,—
Vain the proud homage of our thrall, the sea,
If we be shorn of God:—ah! loathsome shame!
To hurl in battle for the pride of arms:
To ride in native tournay, foreign war:
To count the stars; to ponder pictured runes,—
And grasp great knowledge, as the demons do,—
If we be shorn of God:—we must assay
The myth and meaning of this marvellous bowl:
It shall be sought and found:—"
       Thus said the King.

Then rose a storm of voices! like the sea,—
When Ocean bounding, shouts with all his waves!
High-hearted men: the purpose and the theme,
Smote the fine chord that thrills the warrior's soul,
With touch and impulse for a deed of fame.

Then spake Sir Gauvain, counsellor of the King,—
A man of Pentecost for words that burn:—

"Sirs! we are soldiers of the rock and ring:
Our table-round is earth's most honoured stone,—
Thereon two worlds of life and glory blend!
The boss upon the shield of many a land:
The midway link with light beyond the stars!
This is our fount of fame! let us arise,
And cleave the earth like rivers: like the streams
That win from Paradise their immortal name:
To the four winds of God! casting the lot.

"So shall we share the regions! and unfold
The shrouded mystery of those fields of air.

"Eastward! the source and spring of life and light:
Thence came, and thither went, the rush of worlds,
When the great cone of space [a] was sown with stars!
There rolled the gateway of the double dawn,

---

[a] Space is a created thing, material and defined. As time is *mensura motus*, so is space *mensura loci;* and it signifies that part of God's presence which is measured out to enfold the planetary universe. The tracery of its outline is a cone. Every path of a planet is a curve of that conic figure: and as motion is the life of matter, the whirl of space in its allotted courses is the cause of that visible movement of the sun and the solar system towards the star Alcyone as the fixed centre in the cone o space.

When the mere God shone down a breathing man!
There, up from Bethany, the Syrian Twelve,
Watched their dear Master darken into day!
Thence too will gleam the Cross, the arisen wood º :
Ah, shuddering sign one day of terrible doom!
Therefore the Orient is the home of God.

" The West! a Galilee: the shore of men!
The symbol and the scene of populous life:
Full Japhet journeyed thither, Noe's son,
The prophecy of increase in his loins.
Westward ᵖ Lord Jesu looked His latest love,—
His yearning Cross along the peopled sea,
The innumerable nations in His soul:
Thus came that type and token of our kind,
The realm and region of the set of sun,
The wide wide West: the imaged zone of man.

" The North! the lair of demons, where they coil,
And bound, and glide, and travel to and fro:

  º The " Sign of the Son of Man," the signal of the last day, was understood, in the early ages, to denote the actual Cross of Calvary; which was to be miraculously recalled into existence, and, angel-borne, to announce the advent of the Lord in the sky.
  ᵖ Our Lord was crucified with His back towards the east: His face therefore was turned towards the west, which is always in sacred symbolism the region of the people.

Their gulph, the underworld, this hollow orb,
Where vaulted columns curve beneath the hills
And shoulder us on their arches: there they throng:
The portal of their pit, the polar gate;
Their fiery dungeon mocked with northern snow:
There doom and demon haunt a native land,
Where dreamy thunder mutters in the cloud,
Storm broods, and battle breathes, and baleful fires
Shed a fierce horror o'er the shuddering North!

"But thou! O South Wind, breathe thy fragrant sigh:
We follow on thy perfume, breath of heaven!
Myriads, in girded albs, for ever young,
Their stately semblance of embodied air,
Troop round the footstool of the Southern Cross;
That pentacle of stars: the very sign
That led the Wise Men towards the aweful Child,—
Then came and stood to rule the peaceful sea!
So too Lord Jesu from His mighty tomb [q],
Cast the dear shadow of His red right hand,
To soothe the happy South: the angels' home.

---

[q] Our Lord was laid in His sepulchre with His head toward the west: His right hand therefore gave symbolic greeting to the region of the south, as His left hand reproached and gave a fatal aspect to the north.

"Then let us search the regions! one by one,
And pluck this Sangraal from its cloudy cave."

So Merlin brought the arrows: graven lots,
Shrouded from sight within a quivered sheath,
For choice and guidance in the perilous path,
That so the travellers might divide the lands.

They met at Lauds, in good Saint Nectan's Cell,
For fast, and vigil, and their knightly vow:
Then knelt, and prayed, and all received their God.

"Now, for the silvery arrows, grasp and hold!"

Sir Lancelot drew the North: that fell domain,
Where fleshly man must brook the airy fiend,—
His battle foe, the demon: ghastly war!
Ho! stout Saint Michael shield them, knight and
    knave.

The South fell softly to Sir Perceval's hand:
Some shadowy angel breathed a silent sign:
That so that blameless man, that courteous knight
Might mount and mingle with the happy host
Of God's white army in their native land!
Yea, they shall woo and soothe him, like the dove.

But hark! the greeting! "Tristan for the West!"

Among the multitudes, his watchful way:
The billowy hordes beside the seething sea;
But will the glory gleam in loathsome lands?
Will the lost pearl shine out among the swine?
Woe, Father Adam, to thy loins and thee.

Sir Galahad holds the Orient arrow's name:
His chosen hand unbars the gate of day!
There glows that heart, filled with his mother's blood,
That rules in every pulse, the world of man;
Link of the aweful Three, with many a star.
O! blessed East! 'mid visions such as thine,
'Twere well to grasp the Sangraal, and die.

Now feast and festival in Arthur's hall:
Hark! stern Dundagel softens into song!
They meet for solemn severance, knight and king:
Where gate and bulwark darken o'er the sea.
Strong men for meat, and warriors at the wine:
They wreak the wrath of hunger on the beeves,—
They rend rich morsels from the savoury deer,—
And quench the flagon like Brun-guillie[r] dew!

[r] The golden-hill, from *brun*, 'a hill,' and *guillie*, 'golden:' so called from the yellow gorse with which it is clothed.

Hear! how the minstrels prophesy in sound.
Shout the King's Waes-hael, and Drink-hael the
    Queen.

Then said Sir Kay, he of the arrowy tongue,
"Joseph and Pharaoh! how they build their bones!
Happier the boar were quick than dead to-day."

The Queen! the Queen! how haughty on the dais;
The sunset tangled in her golden hair:
A dove amid the eagles: Gwennivar!
Aishah! what might is in that glorious eye!
See their tamed lion [s] from Brocelian's glade,
Couched on the granite like a captive king,—
A word—a gesture—or a mute caress,
How fiercely fond he droops his billowy mane,
And wooes, with tawny lip, his lady's hand.

The dawn is deep: the mountains yearn for day;
The hooting cairn [t] is hushed: that fiendish noise,

---

  [s] This appropriate fondling of the knights of Dundagel moves Villemarque to write, "Qui me plaise et me charme quand je le trouve couché aux pieds d'Ivain le mufle allongé sur ses deux pattes croiseés les yeux à demi ouvert et revant."

  [t] See Borlase, book iii. ch. 3. for "Karn-idzck;" touched by the moon at some weird hour of the night, it hooted with oracular sound.

Yelled from the utterance of the rending rock,
When the fierce dog of Cain barks from the moon [u].

The bird of judgment chants the doom of night:
The billows laugh a welcome to the day,
And Camlan ripples, seaward, with a smile.

"Down with the eastern bridge! the warriors ride,
And thou, Sir Herald, blazon as they pass!"

Foremost sad Lancelot, throned upon his steed,
His yellow banner, northward, lapping light:
The crest, a lily, with a broken stem,
The legend, Stately once and ever fair;
It hath a meaning, seek it not, O king!

A quaint embroidery Sir Perceval wore;
A turbaned Syrian, underneath a palm,
Wrestled for mastery with a stately foe,
Robed in a Levite's raiment, white as wool:
His touch o'erwhelmed the Hebrew, and his word,
Whoso is strong with God shall conquer man,
Coiled in rich tracery round the knightly shield.
Did Ysolt's delicate fingers weave the web,
That gleamed in silken radiance o'er her lord?

[u] Cain and his dog: Dante's version of the man in the moon was a thought of the old simplicity of primeval days.

A molten rainbow, bent; that arch in heaven,
Which leads straightway to Paradise and God;
Beneath, came up a gloved and sigilled hand,
Amid this cunning needlework of words,
𝔚𝔥𝔢𝔫 𝔱𝔬𝔦𝔩 𝔞𝔫𝔡 𝔱𝔢𝔞𝔯𝔰 𝔥𝔞𝔳𝔢 𝔴𝔬𝔯𝔫 𝔱𝔥𝔢 𝔴𝔢𝔰𝔱𝔢𝔯𝔦𝔫𝔤 𝔡𝔞𝔶,
𝔅𝔢𝔥𝔬𝔩𝔡 𝔱𝔥𝔢 𝔰𝔪𝔦𝔩𝔢 𝔬𝔣 𝔣𝔞𝔪𝔢! 𝔰𝔬 𝔟𝔯𝔦𝔢𝔣: 𝔰𝔬 𝔟𝔯𝔦𝔤𝔥𝔱.

A vast archangel floods Sir Galahad's shield:
Mid-breast, and lifted high, an Orient cruse,
Full filled, and running o'er with Numynous[x] light,
As though it held and shed the visible God;
Then shone this utterance as in graven fire,
𝔈 𝔱𝔥𝔦𝔯𝔰𝔱! 𝔒 𝔍𝔢𝔰𝔲! 𝔩𝔢𝔱 𝔪𝔢 𝔡𝔯𝔦𝔫𝔨 𝔞𝔫𝔡 𝔡𝔦𝔢!

So forth they fare, King Arthur and his men;
Like stout quaternions of the Maccabee:
They halt, and form at craggy Carradon;
Fit scene for haughty hope and stern farewell.

---

[x] When the cone of space had been traced out and defined, the next act of creation was to replenish it with that first and supernatural element which I have named Numyne. The forefathers called it the spiritual or ethereal element, *cælum;* from Genesis i. 2. Within its texture the other and grosser elements of light and air, ebb and flow, cling and glide. Therein dwell the forces, and thereof angels and all spiritual things receive their substance and form.

Lo! the rude altar; and the rough-hewn rock;
The grim and ghastly semblance of the fiend:
His haunt and coil within that pillared home.
Hark, the wild echo! did the demon breathe
That yell of vengeance from the conscious stone?

There the brown barrow curves its sullen breast,
Above the bones of some dead Gentile's soul:
All hushed—and calm—and cold—until anon
Gleams the old dawn—the well-remembered day—
Then may you hear, beneath that hollow cairn,
The clash of arms: the muffled shout of war;
Blent with the rustle of the kindling dead.

They stand—and hush their hearts to hear the King.

Then said he, like a prince of Tamar-land,
Around his soul, Dundagel and the sea:

"Ha! Sirs—ye seek a noble crest to-day,
To win and wear the starry Sangraal,
The link that binds to God a lonely land.
Would that my arm went with you, like my heart!
But the true shepherd must not shun the fold:
For in this flock are crouching grievous wolves,
And chief among them all, my own false kin.
Therefore I tarry by the cruel sea,

To hear at eve the treacherous mermaid's song,
And watch the wallowing monsters of the wave,
'Mid all things fierce, and wild, and strange, alone.

"Ay! all beside can win companionship:
The churl may clip his mate beneath the thatch,
While his brown urchins nestle at his knees:
The soldier give and grasp a mutual palm,
Knit to his flesh in sinewy bonds of war:
The knight may seek at eve his castle gate,
Mount the old stair, and lift the accustomed latch,
To find, for throbbing brow and weary limb,
That paradise of pillows, one true breast:
But he, the lofty ruler of the land,
Like yonder Tor, first greeted by the dawn,
And woo'd the latest by the lingering day,
With happy homes and hearths beneath his breast,
Must soar and gleam in solitary snow!
The lonely one is evermore the king.
So now farewell, my lieges, fare ye well,
And God's sweet Mother be your benison!
Since by gray Merlin's gloss, this wondrous cup
Is, like the golden vase in Aaron's ark,
A fount of manha for a yearning world,
As full as it can hold of God and heaven:

Search the four winds until the balsam breathe,
Then grasp, and fold it in your very soul!

"I have no son, no daughter of my loins,
To breathe, 'mid future men, their father's name:
My blood will perish when these veins are dry:
Yet am I fain some deeds of mine should live,—
I would not be forgotten in this land:
I yearn that men I know not, men unborn,
Should find, amid these fields, King Arthur's fame!
Here let them say, by proud Dundagel's walls,—
They brought the Sangraal back by his command,
They touched these rugged rocks with hues of God:
So shall my name have worship, and my land!

"Ah! native Cornwall! throned upon the hills:
Thy moorland pathways worn by angel feet,
Thy streams that march in music to the sea
'Mid Ocean's merry noise, his billowy laugh!
Ah me! a gloom falls heavy on my soul,—
The birds that sung to me in youth are dead;—
I think, in dreamy vigils of the night,
It may be God is angry with my land:
Too much athirst for fame: too fond of blood,
And all for earth, for shadows, and the dream
To glean an echo from the winds of song!

"But now, let hearts be high: the Archangel held
A tournay with the fiend on Abarim,
And good Saint Michael won his dragon crest.

"Be this our cry! the battle is for God!
If bevies of foul fiends withstand your path,—
Nay, if strong angels hold the watch and ward,
Plunge in their midst, and shout 'a Sangraal!'"

He ceased; the warriors bent a knightly knee,
And touched with kiss and sign Excalibur;
Then turned and mounted for their perilous way!

That night Dundagel shuddered into storm!
The deep foundations shook beneath the sea:
Yet there they stood, beneath the murky moon,
Above the bastion, Merlin and the King.
Thrice waved the sage his staff: and thrice they saw
A peopled vision throng the rocky moor!

First fell a gloom, thick as a thousand nights,
A pall that hid whole armies; and beneath,
Stormed the wild tide of war: until on high
Gleamed red the dragon, and the Keltic glaive
Smote the loose battle of the roving Dane!
Then yelled a fiercer fight: for brother blood
Rushed mingling; and twin dragons fought the field!

The grisly shadows of his faithful knights
Perplexed their lord: and in their midst, behold!
His own stern semblance waved a phantom-brand,
Drooped, and went down the war:—then cried the
    King,
"Ho! Arthur to the rescue!" and half drew
Excalibur—but sank, and fell entranced!

A touch aroused the monarch: and there stood
He, of the billowy beard and aweful eye,
The ashes of whole ages on his brow,
Merlin the bard: son of a demon-sire!
High, like Ben Amram at the thirsty rock,
He raised his prophet staff: that runic rod,
The stem of Igdrasil *y*—the crutch of Raun—
And wrote strange words along the conscious air.

Forth gleamed the east, and yet it was not day:
A white and glowing horse outrode the dawn;
A youthful rider ruled the bounding rein,
And he, in semblance of Sir Galahad shone:
A vase he held on high; one molten gem,

---

  y Igdrasil, the mystic tree, the ash of the Keltic ritual. The raun or rowan is also the ash of the mountain, another magic wood of the northern nations.

Like massive ruby or the chrysolite:
Thence gushed the light in flakes; and flowing, fell
As though the pavement of the sky brake up,
And stars were shed to sojourn on the hills,
From gray Morwenna's stone to Michael's tor,
Until the rocky land was like a heaven.

Then saw they that the mighty quest was won:
The Sangraal swooned along the golden air:
The sea breathed balsam, like Gennesaret:
The streams were touched with supernatural light:
And fonts of Saxon rock, stood, full of God!
Altars arose, each like a kingly throne,
Where the royal chalice, with its lineal blood,
The glory of the presence, ruled and reigned.

This lasted long: until the white horse fled,
The fierce fangs of the libbard in his loins:
Whole ages glided in that blink of time,
While Merlin and the King, looked, wondering, on.

But see! once more the wizard-wand arise,
To cleave the air with signals, and a scene.

Troops of the demon-north, in yellow garb,
The sickly hue of vile Iscariot's hair,
Mingle with men, in unseen multitudes!
Unscared, they throng the valley and the hill;

The shrines were darkened and the chalice void:
That which held God was gone: Maran-atha:
The aweful shadows of the Sangraal, fled!
Yet giant men arose, that seemed as gods,
Such might they gathered from the swarthy kind:
The myths were rendered up, and one by one,
The fire—the light—the air—were tamed and bound
Like votive vassals at their chariot wheel!
Then learnt they war, yet not that noble wrath,
That brings the generous champion face to face,
With equal shield, and with a measured brand,
To peril life for life, and do or die!
But the false valour of the lurking fiend,—
To hurl a distant death from some deep den:
To wing with flame the metal of the mine:
And, so they rend God's image, reck not who.

"Ah! haughty England! lady of the wave!"
Thus said pale Merlin to the listening King:—
"What is thy glory in the world of stars?
"To scorch and slay: to win demoniac fame,
In arts and arms; and then to flash and die.
Thou art the diamond of the demon crown,
Smitten by Michael upon Abarim,
That fell; and glared, an island of the sea.
Ah! native England! wake thine ancient cry:

'Ho! for the Sangraal! vanished vase of heaven!
That held, like Christ's own heart, an hin of blood.'"

He ceased: and all around was dreamy night:
There stood Dundagel, throned; and the great sea
Lay, a strong vassal at his master's gate,
And, like a drunken giant, sobbed in sleep.

Pompeii.

How fair the scene! the sunny smiles of day
Flash o'er the wave in glad Sorrento's bay;
Far, far along mild Sarno's glancing stream,
The fruits and flowers of golden summer beam,
And cheer, with brightning hues, the lonely gloom,
That shrouds yon silent City of the Tomb!
Yes, sad Pompeii! Time's deep shadows fall
On every ruined arch and broken wall;
But Nature smiles as in thy happiest hour,
And decks thy lowly rest with many a flower.
Around, above, in blended beauty shine
The graceful poplar and the clasping vine;
Still the young violet[a], in her chalice blue,
Bears to the lip of Morn her votive dew;
Still the green laurel springs to life the while,
Beneath her own Apollo's golden smile;
And o'er thy fallen beauties beams on high
The glory of the heavens—Italia's sky!

[a] The violets of this district are proverbial for their abundance and beauty.

How fair the scene! e'en now to Fancy's gaze
Return the shadowy forms of other days:
Those halls, of old with mirth and music rife,
Those echoing streets that teemed with joyous life,
The stately towers that looked along the plain,
And the light barks that swept yon silvery main.
And see! they meet beneath the chestnut shades,
Pompeii's joyous sons and graceful maids,
Weave the light dance—the rosy chaplet twine,
Or snatch the cluster from the weary vine;
Nor think that death can haunt so fair a scene,
The Heavens' deep blue, the Earth's unsullied green.

 Devoted City! could not aught avail
When the dark omen [b] told thy fearful tale?
The giant phantom dimly seen to glide,
And the loud voice [c] that shook the mountain-side,
With warning tones that bade thy children roam,
To seek in happier climes a calmer home?

---

 [b] Dio Cassius, lxvi. relates, that, previously to the destruction of the city, figures of gigantic size were seen hovering in the air, and that a voice like the sound of a trumpet was often heard. Probably the imagination of the inhabitants invested with human figure the vapours that preceded the eruption.

 [c] "Vox quoque per lucos vulgo exaudita silentes
  Ingens; et simulacra modis pallentia miris
  Visa sub obscurum noctis." *Virg. Georg.*, i. 476.

In vain! they will not break the fatal rest
That wooes them to the mountain's treacherous
    breast:
Fond memory blends with every mossy stone
Some early joy, some tale of pleasure flown;
And they must die where those around will weep,
And sleep for ever where their fathers sleep.
Yes! they must die: behold! yon gathering gloom
Brings on the fearful silence of the tomb;
Along Campania's sky yon murky cloud
Spreads its dark form—a City's funeral shroud.

    How brightly rose Pompeii's latest day[d]!
The Sun, unclouded, held his golden way,—
Vineyards, in Autumn's purple glories drest,
Slept in soft beauty on the mountain's breast;
The gale that wantoned round his crested brow,
Shook living fragrance from the blossomed bough;
And many a laughing mead and silvery stream
Drank the deep lustre of the noonday beam:
Then echoing Music rang, and Mirth grew loud
In the glad voices of the festal crowd;

---

[d] Pompeii was destroyed on the 23rd of August, A.D. 79. See Plinii Epist., l. vi. 16, 20; Dio Cassius, lxvi. It remained undiscovered during fifteen centuries.

The opening Theatre's ᵉ wide gates invite,
The choral dance is there, the solemn rite—
There breathes th' immortal Muse her spell around,
And swelling thousands flood the fated ground.
See! where arise before th' enraptured throng,
The fabled scenes, the shadowy forms of Song!
Gods, that with heroes leave their starry bowers,
Their fragrant hair entwined with radiant flowers,
Haunt the dim grove, beside the fountain dwell—
Strike the deep lyre, or sound the wreathed shell—
With forms of heavenly mould; but hearts that glow
With human passion, melt with human woe:
Breathless they gaze, while white-robed priests advance,
And graceful virgins lead the sacred dance;
They listen, mute, while mingling tones prolong
The lofty accent, and the pealing song,

ᵉ Eustace, and other modern writers, have thought it improbable that the inhabitants of Pompeii could have assembled to enjoy the amusement of the theatre after the shocks of the earthquake and other symptons of danger which preceded the eruption; but as their theatrical representations partook of the nature of religious solemnities, there does not seem sufficient reason to disregard the positive assertion of Dio Cassius to the contrary.

Echo th' unbending Titan's haughty groan,
Or in the Colchian's woes forget their own [f]!
Why feels each throbbing heart that shuddering chill?
The Music falters, and the Dance is still—
" Is it pale twilight stealing o'er the plain?
Or starless Eve, that holds unwonted reign?"
Hark to the thrilling answer! who shall tell
When thick and fast th' unsparing tempest fell,
And stern Vesuvius poured along the vale
His molten cataracts, and his burning hail:
Oh! who shall paint, in that o'erwhelming hour,
Death's varying forms, and Horror's withering power?
Earthquake! wild Earthquake! rends that heaving
    plain,
Cleaves the firm rock, and swells the beetling main:
Here, yawns the ready grave, and, raging, leap
Earth's secret fountains from their troubled sleep;
There, from the quivering mountain bursts on high
The pillared flame, that wars along the sky!
On, on they press, and maddening seek in vain
Some soothing refuge from the fiery rain;—

---

[f] Ivory tickets of admission were found in the vicinity of one of the theatres, inscribed on one side with the name of a play of Æschylus, and on the other with a representation of the theatre itself. One or two of these are preserved in the studio at Naples.

Their home? it can but yield a living tomb,
Round the loved hearth is brooding deepest gloom;
Yon sea? its angry surges scorching rave,
And death-fires gleam upon the ruddy wave:
Oh! for one breath of that reviving gale,
That swept at dewy morn along the vale!
For one sad glance of their beloved sky,
To soothe, though vain, their parting agony!
Yon mother bows in vain her shuddering form,
Her babe to shield from that relentless storm:
Cold are those limbs her clasping arms constrain,
Even the soft shelter of her breast is vain!
Gaze on that form! 'tis Beauty's softest maid,
The rose's rival in her native shade;—
For her had Pleasure reared her fairest bowers,
And Song and Dance had sped the laughing hours:
See! o'er her brow the kindling ashes glow,
And the red shower o'erwhelms her breast of snow;
She seeks that loved one— never false till then;—
She calls on him—who answers not again:
Loose o'er her bosom flames her golden hair,
And every thrilling accent breathes despair!
Even the stern priest, who saw with raptured view,
The deathless forms of Heaven's ethereal blue,

Who drank, with glowing ear, the mystic tone,
That clothed his lips with wonders not their own,
Beheld the immortal marble frown in vain,
And fires triumphant grasp the sacred fane,
Forsook at last the unavailing shrine,
And cursed his faithless gods—no more divine!

 Morn came in beauty still—and shone as fair,
Though cold the hearts that hailed its radiance there,
And Evening, crowned with many a starry gem,
Sent down her softest smile—though not for them!
Where gleamed afar Pompeii's graceful towers,
Where hill and vale were clothed with vintage bowers,
O'er a dark waste the smouldering ashes spread,
A pall above the dying and the dead.

 Still the dim city slept in safest shade,
Though the wild waves another Queen obeyed,
And sad Italia, on her angry shore,
Beheld the North its ruthless myriads pour;
And nature scattered all her treasures round,
And graced with fairest hues the blighted ground.
There oft, at glowing noon, the village maid
Sought the deep shelter of the vineyard shade;
Beheld the olive bud—the wild-flower wave,
Nor knew her step was on a people's grave!

But see! once more beneath the smiles of day,
The dreary mist of ages melts away!
Again Pompeii, 'mid the brightening gloom,
Comes forth in beauty from her lonely tomb.
Lovely in ruin—graceful in decay,
The silent City rears her walls of gray:
The clasping ivy hangs her faithful shade,
As if to hide the wreck that time had made;
The shattered column on the lonely ground,
Is glittering still, with fresh acanthus crowned;
And where her Parian rival moulders near,
The drooping lily pours her softest tear!
How sadly sweet with pensive step to roam
Amid the ruined wall, the tottering dome!
The path just worn by human feet is here;
Their echoes almost reach the listening ear:
The marble halls with rich mosaic drest;
The portal wide that wooes the lingering guest:
Altars, with fresh and living chaplets crowned,
From those wild flowers that spring fantastic
    round,
The unfinished painting, and the pallet nigh,
Whose added hues must fairer charms supply:
These mingle here, until th' unconscious feet
Roam on, intent some gathering crowd to meet;

And cheated Fancy, in her dreamy mood,
Will half forget that it is solitude!
　Yes, all is solitude! fear not to tread,
Through gates unwatched, the City of the Dead,
Explore with pausing step th' unpeopled path,
View the proud hall—survey the stately bath,
Where swelling roofs their noblest shelter raise;
Enter! no voice shall check th' intruder's gaze!
See! the dread legion's peaceful home is here,
The signs of martial life are scattered near.
Yon helm, unclasped to ease some Warrior's
　　brow,
The sword his weary arm resigned but now,
Th' unfinished sentence traced along the wall,
Broke by the hoarse Centurion's startling call:
Hark! did their sounding tramp re-echo round?
Or breathed the hollow gale that fancied sound?
Behold! where 'mid yon fane, so long divine,
Sad Isis mourns her desolated shrine!
Will none the mellow reed's soft music breathe?
Or twine from yonder flowers the victim's wreath?
None to yon altar lead with suppliant strain
The milk-white monarch of the herd again [g]?

　　[g] "Hinc alibi, Clitumne, greges, et maxima taurus
　　　　Victima."　*Virg. Georg.*, ii. 146.

All, all is mute! save sadly answering nigh
The nightbird's shriek, the shrill cicada's cry.
Yet may you trace along the furrowed street,
The chariot's track—the print of frequent feet;
The gate unclosed, as if by recent hand;
The hearth, where yet the guardian Lares stand;
Still on the walls the words of welcome shine [h],
And ready vases proffer joyous wine [i]:
But where the hum of men? the sounds of life?
The Temple's pageant, and the Forum's strife?
The forms and voices, such as should belong
To that bright clime, the land of Love and Song?
How sadly echoing to the stranger's tread,
These walls respond, like voices from the dead!
And sadder traces—darker scenes are there,
Tales of the Tomb, and records of Despair;
In Death's chill grasp unconscious arms enfold
The fatal burden of their cherished gold [k];
Here, wasted relics, as in mockery, dwell
Beside some treasure loved in life too well;

[h] On many of the walls the word *Salve* is carved over the door.

[i] "The amphoræ which contained wine still remain, and the marble slabs are marked with cups and glasses."—*Eustace.*

[k] "At the door of the court of one of the houses skeletons were found, one with a key, another with a purse."—*Eustace.*

There, faithful hearts have mouldered side by side,
And hands are clasped that Death could not divide!
None, none shall tell that hour of fearful strife,
When Death must share the consciousness of Life;
When sullen Famine, slow Despair consume
The living tenants of the massive tomb;
Long could they hear, above th' incumbent plain,
The music of the breeze awake again,
The wave's deep echo on the distant shore,
And murmuring streams, that they should see no more!
Away! dread scene! and o'er the harrowing view
Let Night's dim shadows fling their darkest hue!

 But there, if still beneath some nameless stone,
By waving weeds and ivy-wreaths o'ergrown,
Lurk the gray spoils of Poet or of Sage,
Tully's deep lore, or Livy's pictured page;
If sweet Menander, where his relics fade,
Mourn the dark refuge of Oblivion's shade;
Oh! may their treasures burst the darkling mine!
Glow in the living voice, the breathing line!
Their vestal fire our midnight lamp illume,
And kindle Learning's torch from sad Pompeii's tomb!

A Canticle for Christmas, 1874.

Lo! a pure Maiden, meek and mild,
Yearns to embrace an aweful Child!
Those limbs, her tenderest touch might win:
Yet thrill they with the God within!

She gazes! and what doth she see?
A gleaming Infant on her knee!
She pauses: can she dare to press,
That Glory, with a fond caress?

Yet, 'tis her Flesh: that Form so fair!
Her very Blood is bounding there!
The Mother's heart the victory won:—
It is her God! It is her Son!

Hers the proud gladness mothers know:
Without a thrill; without a throe;
And Mary—Mary undefiled,
Claims for her breast that aweful Child!

PRINTED BY PARKER AND CO., CROWN YARD, OXFORD.

The Vyvyan Cry.

Shall the grey tower in ruin bow?
Must the babe die with nameless brow?
Or common hands in mockery fling,
The unblessed waters of the spring?
No! while the Cornish voice can ring
The Vyvyan Cry, "Our Church and King!"

Shall the grey tower in ruin stand
When the heart thrills within the hand,
And beauty's lip to youth has given
The vow on Earth that lives for heaven?
Shall no glad peal from Church tower grey
Cheer the young maiden's homeward way?
No! while the Cornish voice can ring,
And Vyvyan Cry, "Our Church and King!"

Shall the grey tower in ruin spread?
And must the furrow hold the dead
Without the toll of passing knell,
Without the stoled priest to tell
Of Christ the first fruits of the dead,
To wake the brother from his bed? —
No! while the Cornish voice can ring,
And Vyvyan Cry, "Our Church and King!"

Sir Richard Vyvyan & Sir C. Lemon were standing for East Cornwall as Conservatives. The opposition party was that of the Dissenters. Their Cry was 'Down with the Church!' On which occasion Hawker wrote the above lines.

Sacred Poetry
PUBLISHED BY PARKER AND CO.
OXFORD, AND 6 SOUTHAMPTON-STREET, STRAND, LONDON.

THE AUTHORIZED EDITIONS OF
THE CHRISTIAN YEAR.
With the Author's latest Corrections and Additions.

NOTICE.—Messrs. PARKER are the sole Publishers of the Editions of the "Christian Year" issued with the sanction and under the direction of the Author's representatives. All Editions without their imprint are unauthorized.

	s.	d.
Small 4to., on toned paper, with red, &c., cloth	10	6
Demy 8vo., cloth	6	0
Foolscap 8vo., cloth	3	6
24mo., red lines, cloth	2	6
32mo., cloth, gilt edges	1	6
32mo., cloth, limp	1	0
48mo., cloth, limp	0	6
Facsimile of the First Edition, 2 vols., 12mo.	7	6

The above Editions (except the Facsimile Edition) are kept in a variety of bindings, which may be ordered through the Trade or the Publishers. The chief bindings are Morocco plain and antique, Calf antique, and Vellum.

By the Author of "The Christian Year."

LYRA INNOCENTIUM. Thoughts in Verse on Christian Children. Twelfth Edition. Fcap. 8vo., cloth, 5s.
———————— 24mo., red lines, cloth, 3s. 6d.
———————— 48mo. edition, limp cloth, 6d.; cloth boards, 1s.

MISCELLANEOUS POEMS. Third Edition. Fcap., cl., 6s.

THE PSALTER, or, Psalms of David: In English Verse. Fourth Edition. Fcap. 8vo., cloth, 6s.
———————— Cheap Edition. 18mo., cloth, 1s.

A CONCORDANCE TO THE "CHRISTIAN YEAR." Fcap. 8vo., toned paper, cloth, 4s.

Poems by the late Isaac Williams.

Re-issue of the Poetical Works of the late Rev. ISAAC WILLIAMS. *Each volume uniform,* 32mo., *cloth, price* 2s. 6d.

THE CATHEDRAL; or, The Catholic and Apostolic Church in England.

THE BAPTISTERY; or, The Way of Eternal Life.

HYMNS TRANSLATED FROM THE PARISIAN BREVIARY.

THE CHRISTIAN SCHOLAR.

THOUGHTS IN PAST YEARS.

The Fcap. 8vo. Editions of the following may also be obtained at the annexed prices.

THE BAPTISTERY. With Plates by BOETIUS A BOLSWERT. Fcap. 8vo., cloth, 7s. 6d.

THE CHRISTIAN SCHOLAR. Fcap. 8vo., cloth, 5s.

THE SEVEN DAYS of the CREATION. Fcap. 8vo., cl., 3s. 6d.

Morning Thoughts.

By a CLERGYMAN. Suggested by the Second Lessons for the Daily Morning Service throughout the Year. 2 vols. Fcap. 8vo., cloth, 5s. each.

Florum Sacra.

SHORT POEMS, by the Rev. G. HUNT SMYTTAN. Second Edition. 16mo., 1s.

Hymns on the Litany.

By A. C. Fcap. 8vo., on toned paper, cloth extra, 3s.

The Child's Christian Year.

Hymns for every Sunday and Holyday throughout the Year. Cheap Edition, 18mo., cloth, 1s.

The Cleveland Psalter.

The Book of Psalms in English Verse, and in Measures suited for Sacred Music. By E. CHURTON, M.A., Archdeacon of Cleveland. Fcap. 8vo., cloth, 7s. 6d.

The Cross, and Verses of Many Years.

By the Rev. CHARLES NEVILE, M.A., Prebendary of Lincoln, and Rector of Fledborough; and MARIA NEVILE. Fcap. 8vo., cloth, 7s. 6d.

Coxe's Christian Ballads.

CHRISTIAN BALLADS AND POEMS. By ARTHUR CLEVELAND COXE, D.D., Bishop of Western New York. A New Edition. Fcap. 8vo., cloth, 3s. Also selected Poems in a packet, 32mo., 1s.

Hymns on the Imitation of Christ.

THE INNER LIFE. HYMNS on the "Imitation of Christ" by THOMAS A'KEMPIS; designed especially for Use at Holy Communion. By the Author of "Thoughts from a Girl's Life," &c. Fcap. 8vo., cloth, 3s.

Church Poetry.

FAITH: a Poem in Four Books, by LEWIS GIDLEY. Fcap. 8vo., cloth, 3s. 6d.

The Bells of Botteville Tower:

A Christmas Story in Verse: and other Poems. By FREDERICK GEORGE LEE, Author of "The Martyrs of Vienne and Lyons," &c. Fcap. 8vo., cloth, 4s. 6d.

MISCELLANEOUS POEMS.

The English Cavaliers.

LAYS OF THE ENGLISH CAVALIERS. By JOHN J. DANIELL, Perpetual Curate of Langley Fitzurse, Wilts. Small 4to., printed on toned paper, with Frontispiece and Vignette, ornamental cloth extra, gilt edges, 3s.

Poems:

By LEWIS GIDLEY. Post 8vo., cloth, 3s.

Poems:

By the late Rev. SAMUEL RICKARDS, M.A., Rector of Stowlangtoft. Fcap. 8vo., toned paper, cloth, 3s. 6d.

Poems:

By CHARLES H. HOOLE, Student of Christ Church, Oxford. New Edition. Fcap. 8vo., cloth, 6s.

Inter Flumina.

Verses written among Rivers. By the Rev. A. M. MORGAN. Crown 8vo., cloth, 3s. 6d.

OXFORD AND LONDON: PARKER AND CO.